FIELDS OF RESILIENCE

Stories of Strength, Sustainability, and Spirit in Uganda

by
JANELLE
NIGHTINGALE

FIELDS OF RESILIENCE

Stories of Strength, Sustainability, and Spirit in Uganda

Copyright © Janelle Nightingale, 2025

Photos copyright © Janelle Nightingale, 2023

Graphic design by Rossi Spasova

Edited by K.J. Wetherholt

80% of proceeds from this book support Agri Planet Africa through
Agri Planet Foundation, Inc. (EIN: 33-4457313), a 501(c)(3) nonprofit organization. Learn more at agriplanetfoundation.org

For the resilient hearts
whose strength reminds us
that even from the hardest ground,
beauty can rise.

CONTENTS

Contents

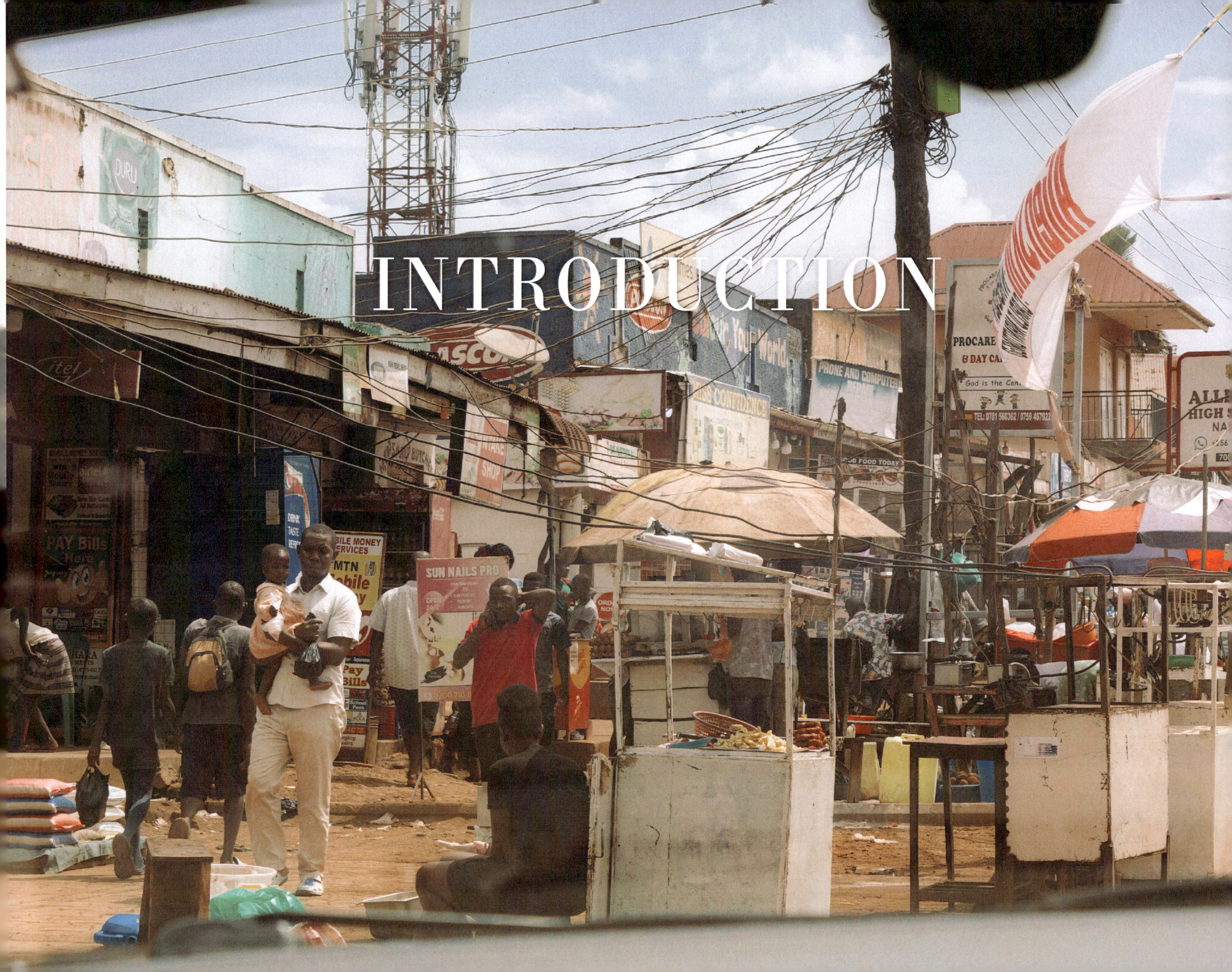
INTRODUCTION

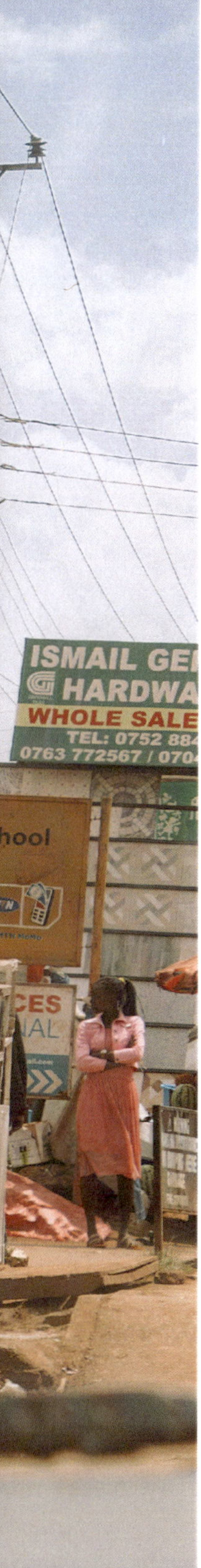

Uganda is not just a place you visit. It's a place that reaches into your soul and plants something enduring there.

When my daughter Lena and I first set foot on Ugandan soil, we thought we were coming to help. But we quickly realized: Uganda was helping us— teaching us about endurance, community, and the quiet power of connection.

Our journey began with uncertainty: rerouted flights, late-night arrivals, unfamiliar roads under velvet skies. Yet by morning, as the first golden light touched Lake Victoria, fear softened into awe, and awe into belonging. Uganda's beauty is immediate, but it is the spirit of its people that lingers long after you leave.

Uganda, the "Pearl of Africa," sits astride the equator with panoramic mountains, vast lakes, and forests that once covered 24% of the land. Today, only 8% remains. Climate change brings longer droughts and unpredictable rains. A growing population of 47 million people puts pressure on the land. Yet Uganda also hosts 1.6 million refugees— more than any African country—with a generosity that amazes the world.

Throughout this book, you'll encounter names written in a way that honors Ugandan tradition: family names appear first, followed by given names. You may also notice *Empaako* names—special "pet names" used among certain communities like the Banyoro, Batooro, and Bafumbira peoples. These names, shared in parentheses after the given name where known, are terms of affection and unity, carrying blessings of respect and connection. Not everyone carries an Empaako name, but where they are known, they are included as part of honoring this beautiful cultural heritage.

Receiving my own Empaako name, *Akiiki*, meaning "one who upholds national, community, and family interests with great love, care, kindness, and honesty," was among the greatest honors of my life. It was a welcome not just into a place, but into a shared humanity.

This journey is woven with many such threads: Meeting Ahumuza Ignatius (*Ateenyi*) and Ahaisibwe Cleofash (*Atwoki*), visionary leaders behind Agri Planet Africa; mentoring and then walking alongside them as they grew a dream into a movement; being entrusted with the story of their communities—stories not of pity, but of profound strength. *Fields of Resilience* is not a story of charity. It is a story of strength: strength in the soil, strength in the hands that plant and build, strength in the voices that rise in song.

In these pages, you'll walk through refugee settlements where hope survives against the odds, sit beneath the shade of banana trees tended by orphan hands, and feel the fierce tenderness of communities who refuse to give up on each other.

Every photograph and every word are offered with deepest gratitude to the people who opened their lives to us.

May you see Uganda not through a lens of lack, but through a lens of abundance—of spirit, of perseverance, of unstoppable hope.

Welcome to Uganda. Welcome to *Fields of Resilience*.

This book serves a purpose beyond storytelling. Eighty percent of proceeds support Agri Planet Africa through Agri Planet Foundation, Inc., a 501(c)(3) nonprofit that facilitates donations from the U.S. to fund the sustainable agriculture education and community resilience programs you'll witness in these pages. Learn more at agriplanetfoundation.org.

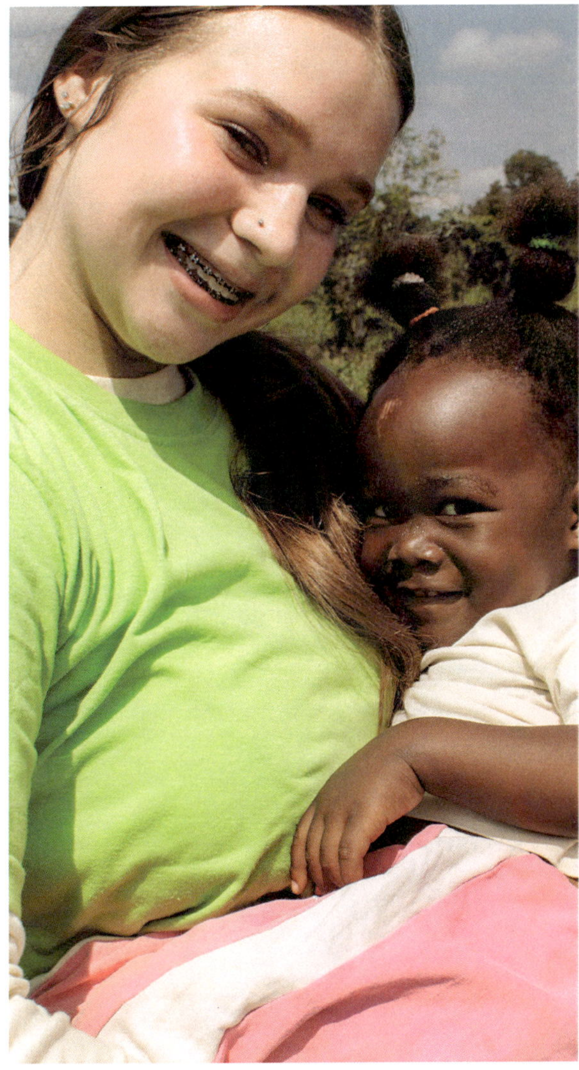
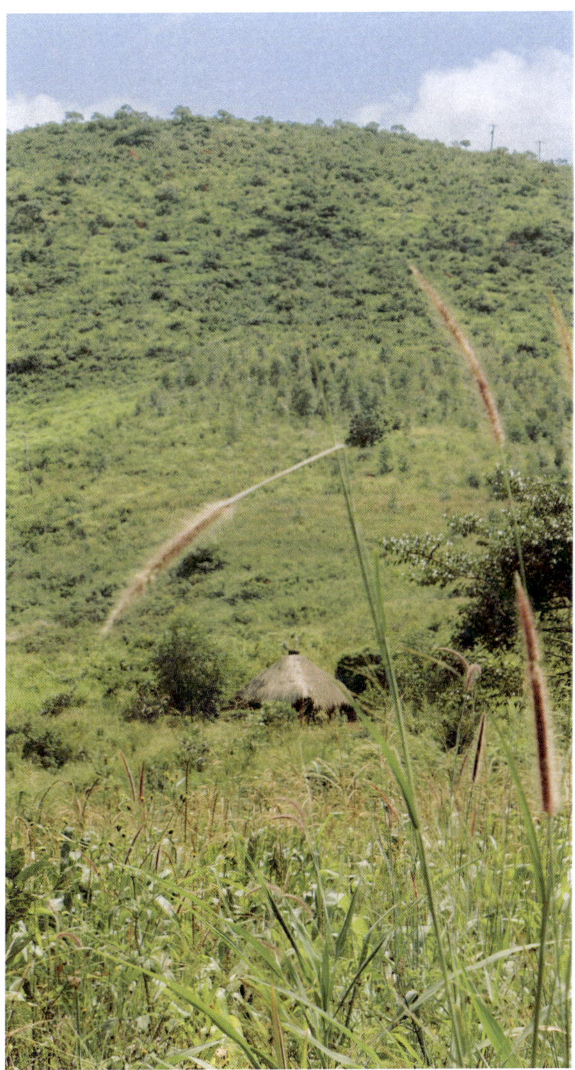
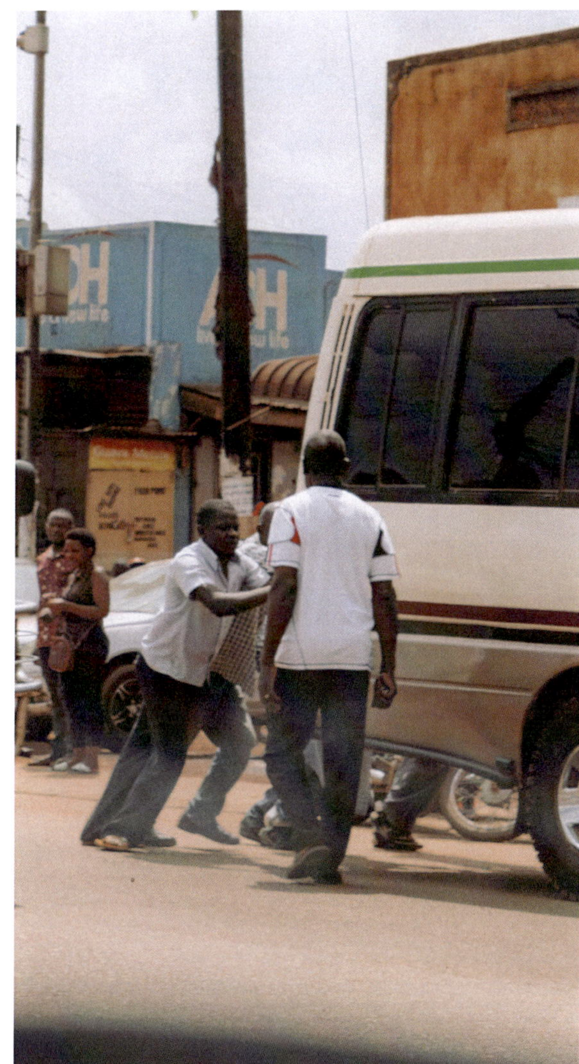

THE HEARTBEAT OF THE WILD

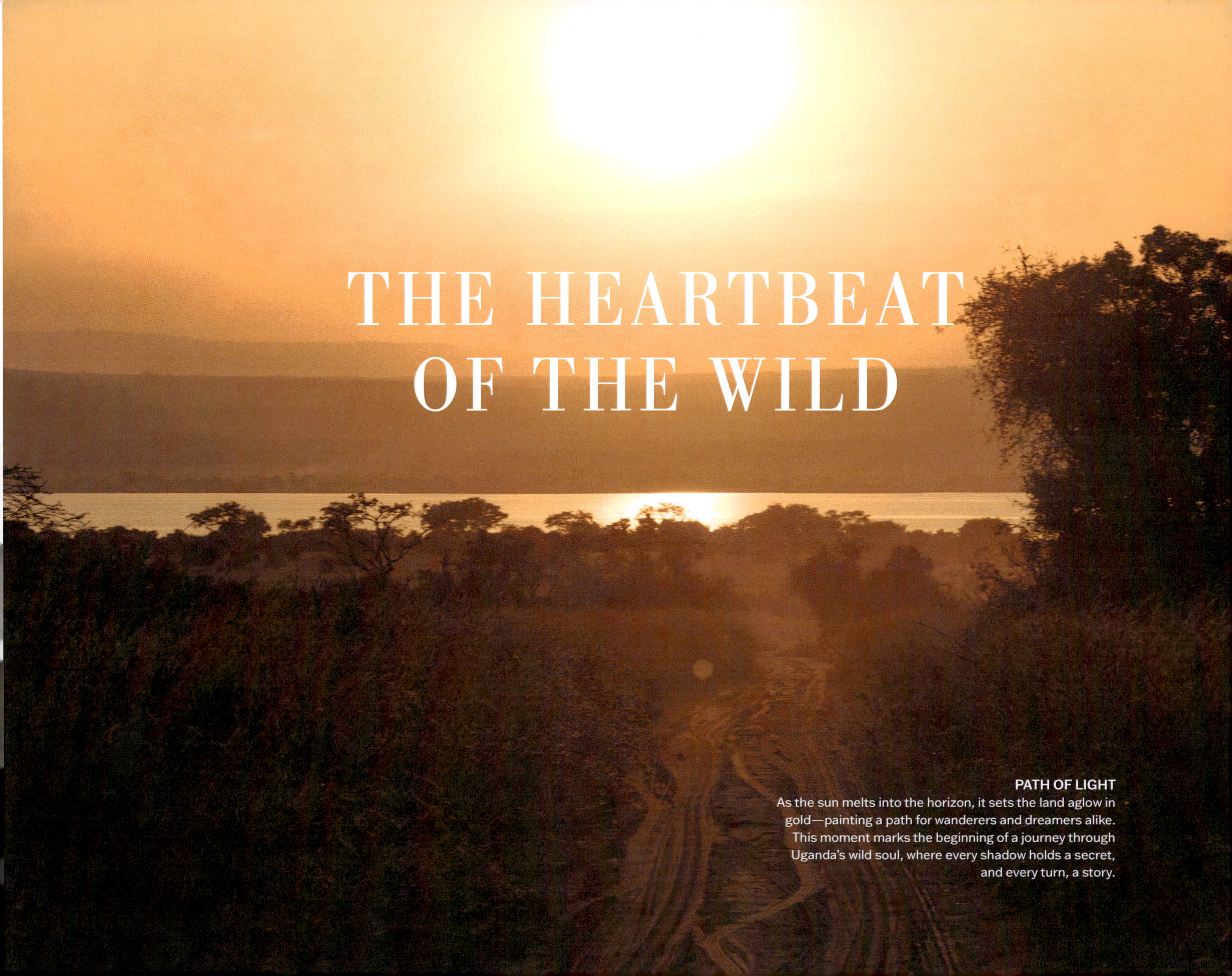

PATH OF LIGHT

As the sun melts into the horizon, it sets the land aglow in gold—painting a path for wanderers and dreamers alike. This moment marks the beginning of a journey through Uganda's wild soul, where every shadow holds a secret, and every turn, a story.

Where Beauty Meets Survival

In the wild heart of Uganda, life pulses with an ancient rhythm, both tender and fierce, breathtaking and unforgiving.

Here, every sunrise paints the savanna in gold, while every shadow holds the delicate dance between predator and prey. This is a land where beauty and survival intertwine like the thorns and blossoms of an acacia tree; each is dependent on the other, each essential to the whole.

From the thunderous power of Murchison Falls to the patient weaving of a bird's nest, from the silent grace of elephants to the watchful eyes of a lion cub learning the ways of the wild, Uganda's wilderness speaks in whispers and roars alike.

This landscape is more than a backdrop; it is the living foundation upon which all stories of survival are built. In every creature's struggle to thrive, in every adaptation born of necessity, we glimpse the same indomitable spirit that flows through the people who call this land home.

But this is not a story of separation… of wilderness on one side and humanity on the other. Here, survival depends on balance: farmers who read the signs of rain and drought, fishermen who understand the language of lake and season, communities who know that their future is bound into the same fabric as the soaring eagle and the patient elephant.

In Uganda, nature and humanity don't merely coexist. They dance together in the endless choreography of harmony.

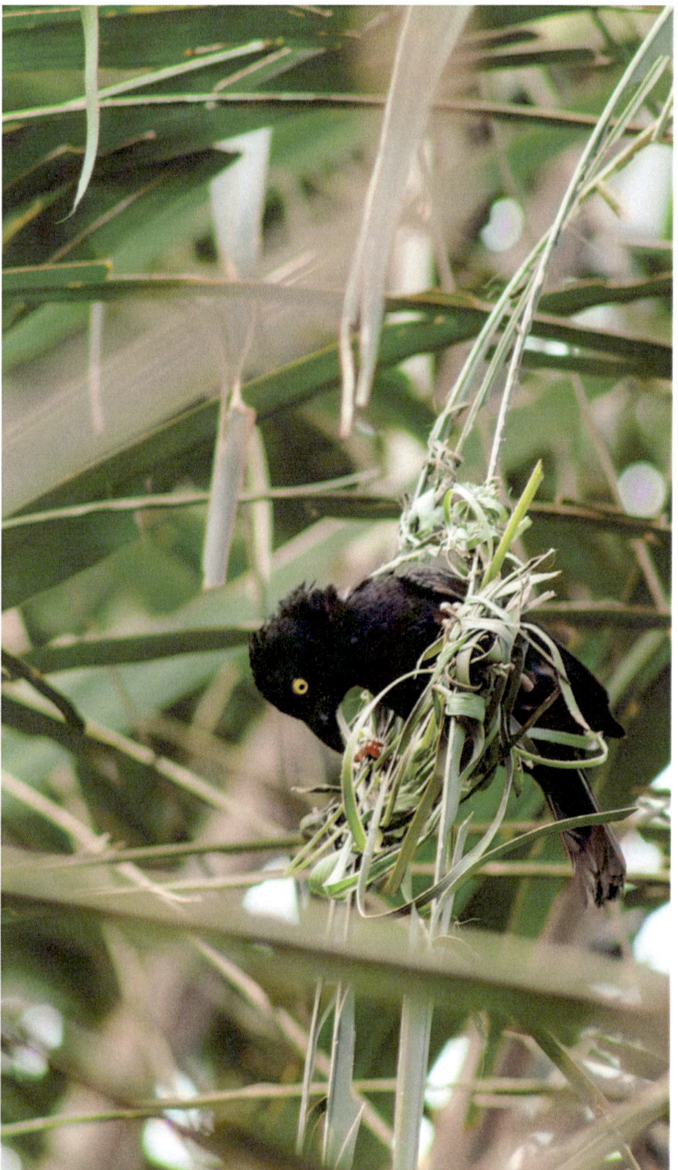

ARCHITECT OF THE WILD

Thread by thread, the weaver bird builds with quiet mastery—its black feathers barely visible among the reeds. Here, survival is an art form, and tenacity is written not in strength, but in the softness of shelter made by instinct and devotion.

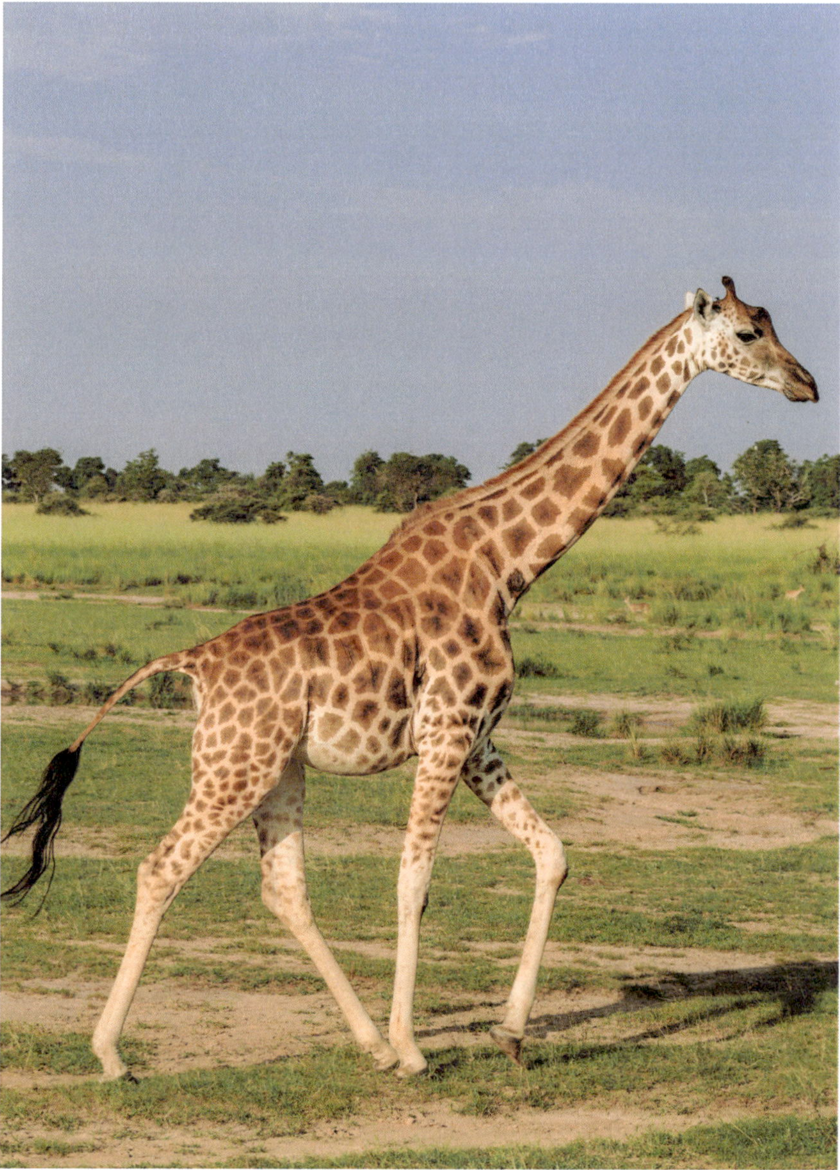

GRACE IN MOTION

Silent and regal, the giraffe moves like a brushstroke across the savanna—its height a monument to evolution's artistry. In its presence, time slows, and the land breathes in harmony—offering a glimpse of balance in a world that rarely stands still.

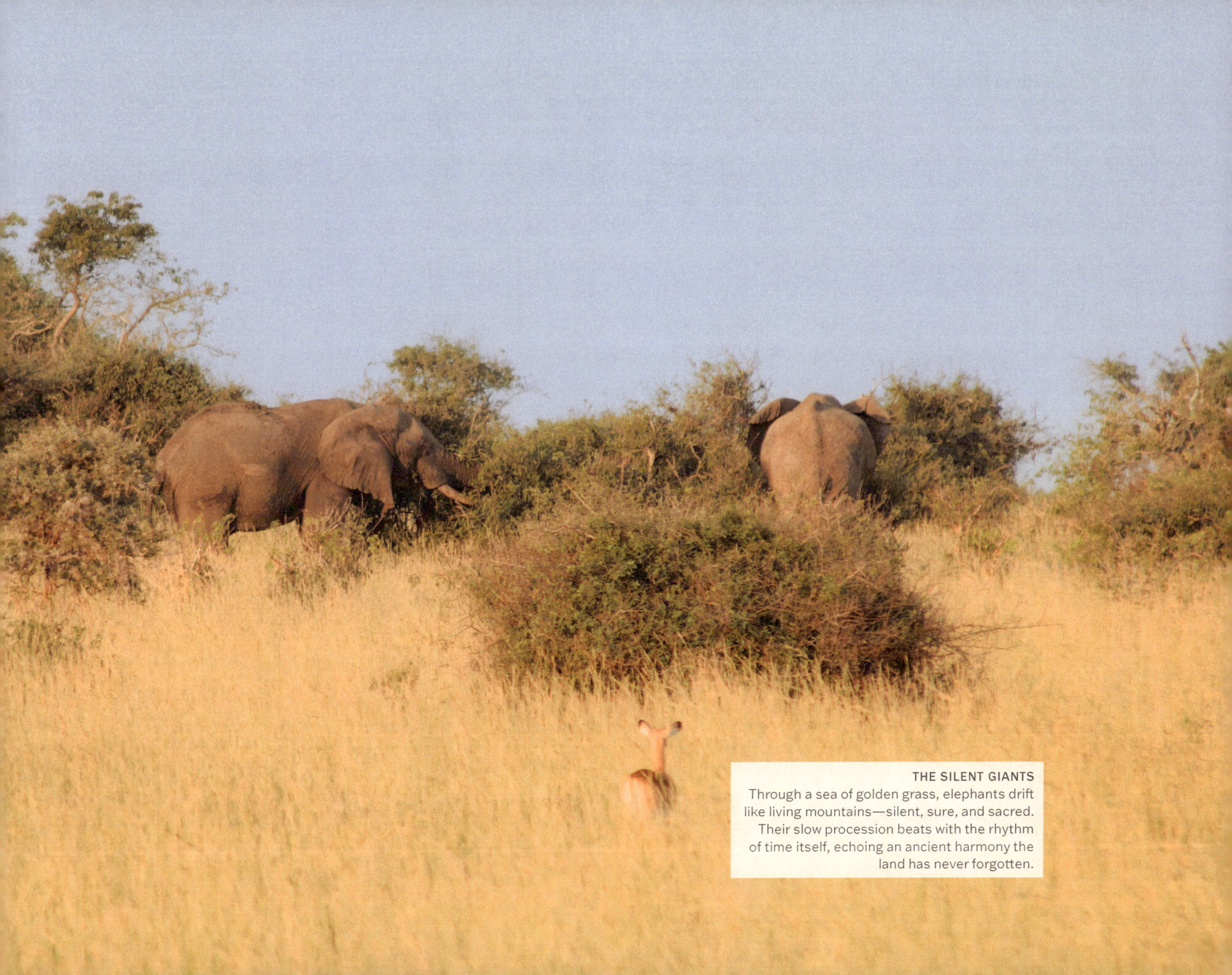

THE SILENT GIANTS
Through a sea of golden grass, elephants drift like living mountains—silent, sure, and sacred. Their slow procession beats with the rhythm of time itself, echoing an ancient harmony the land has never forgotten.

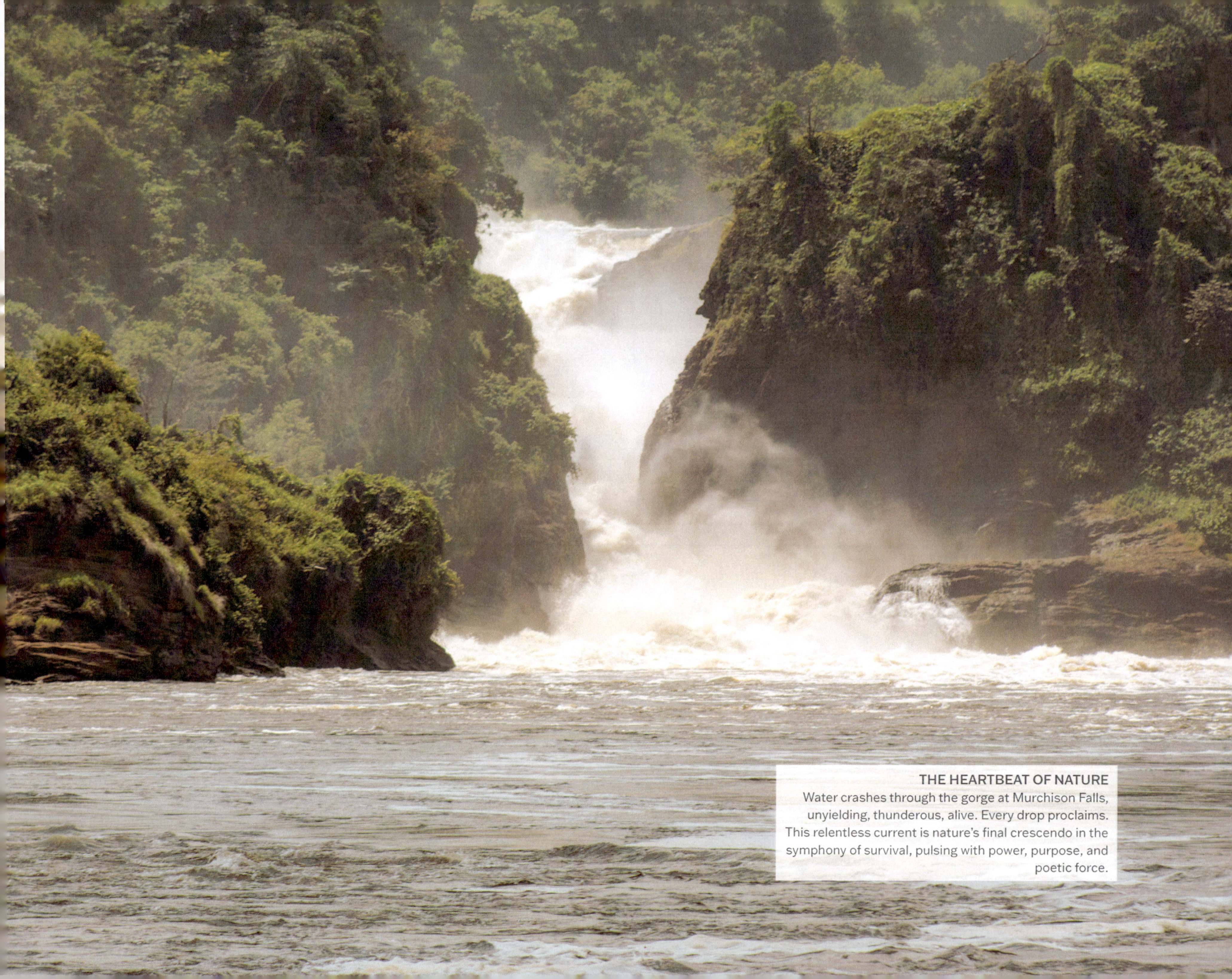

THE HEARTBEAT OF NATURE
Water crashes through the gorge at Murchison Falls, unyielding, thunderous, alive. Every drop proclaims. This relentless current is nature's final crescendo in the symphony of survival, pulsing with power, purpose, and poetic force.

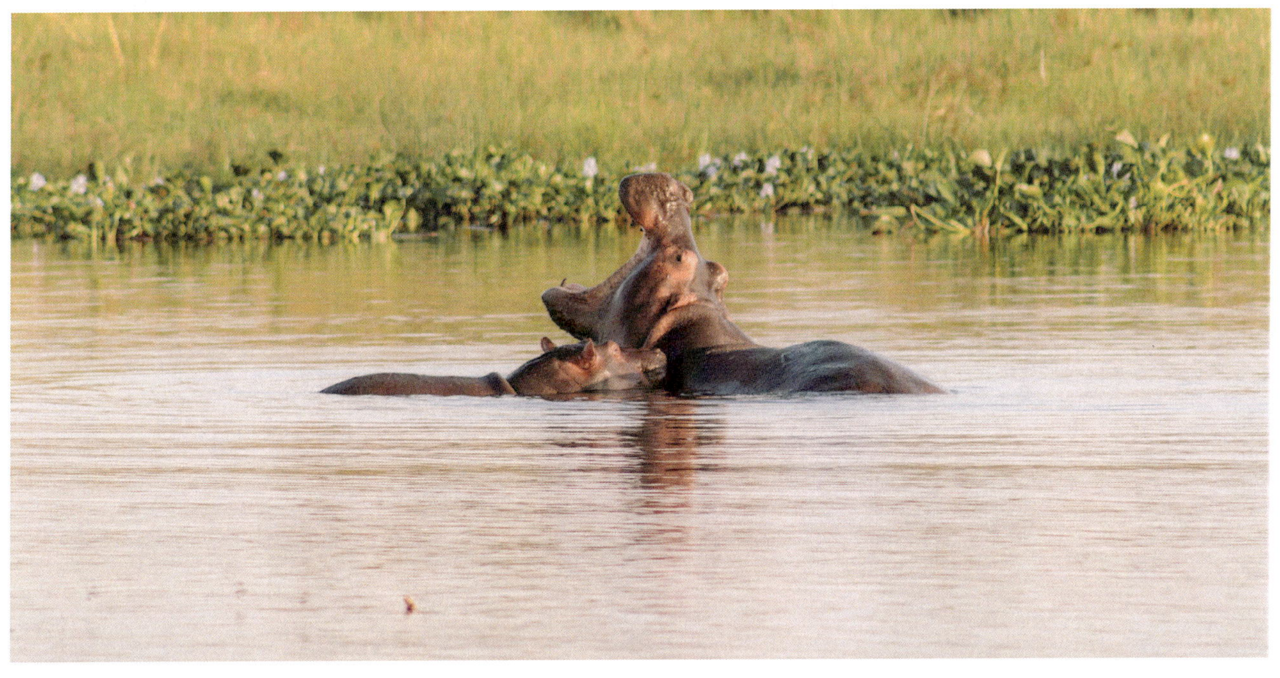

CALM WATERS, HIDDEN POWER

A ripple of the surface, then silence—until the hippo rises, jaws wide in wordless warning. Beneath the stillness flows a primal power, ancient as the river and just as unshakable.

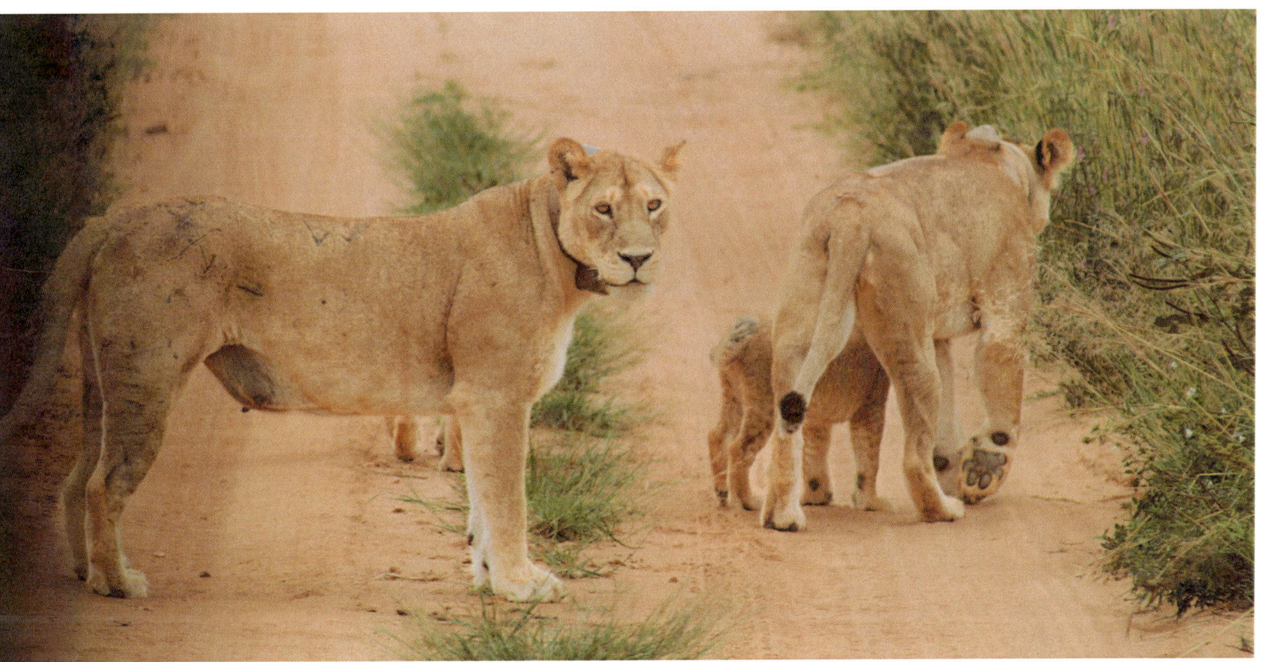

GUARDIANS OF THE PATH

In the hush of the wild, lionesses walk the road of mothers—fierce and watchful. One glances back, eyes soft but sure, her pause a promise: strength and tenderness are not opposites, but companions on the same trail.

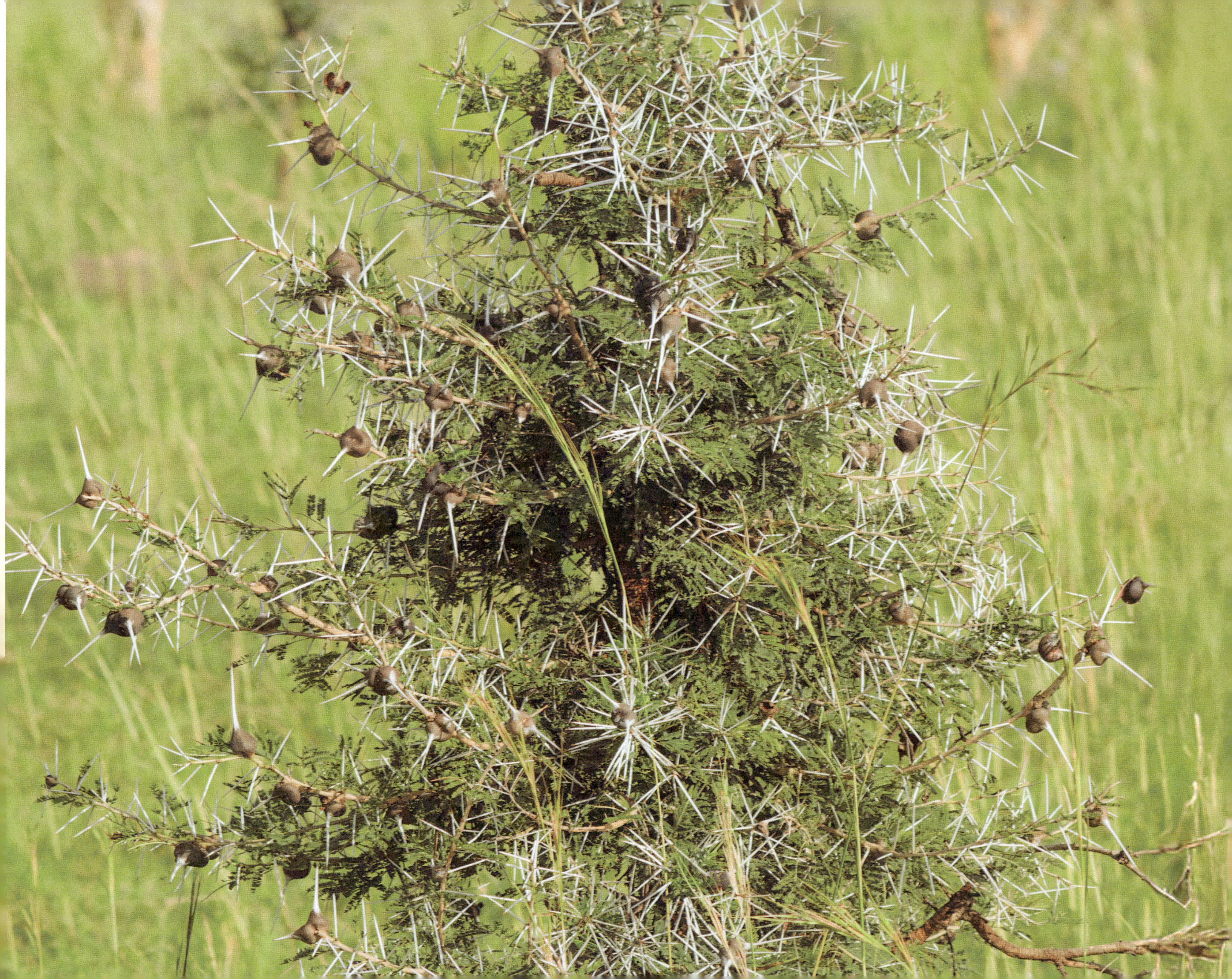

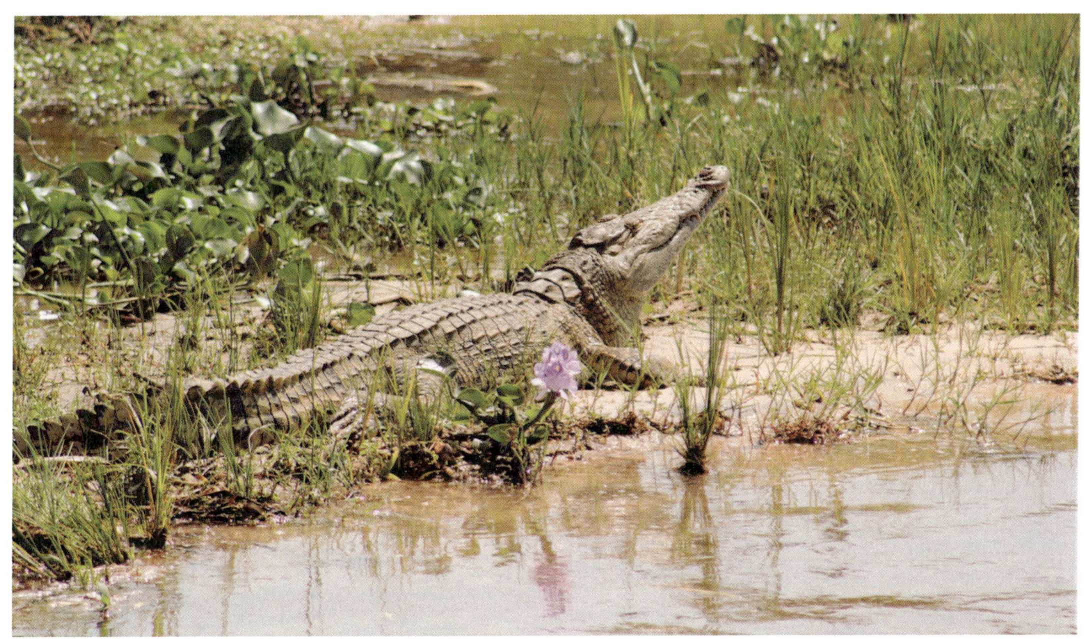

PREDATOR'S PATIENCE

Along the Nile, crocodiles lie unmoving beside a soft purple bloom. Beauty and danger meet in quiet contrast as this stillness concealing ancient instinct, this bloom daring to exist where few others would. Nature, in all her wisdom, holds both life and death in the same breath.

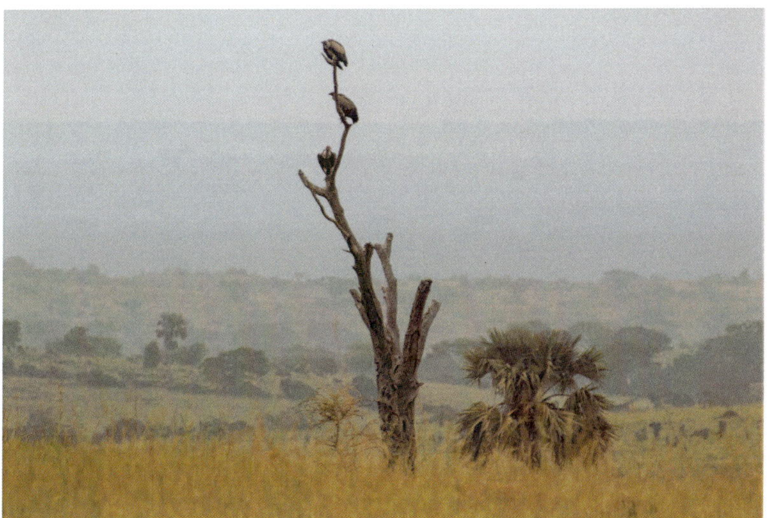

ECHOES IN THE SKY

Perched high above the plains, vultures survey a land that never sleeps. They do not hunt; they watch.
Their wings trace ancient stories across the horizon—stories of what was, and what will come again.

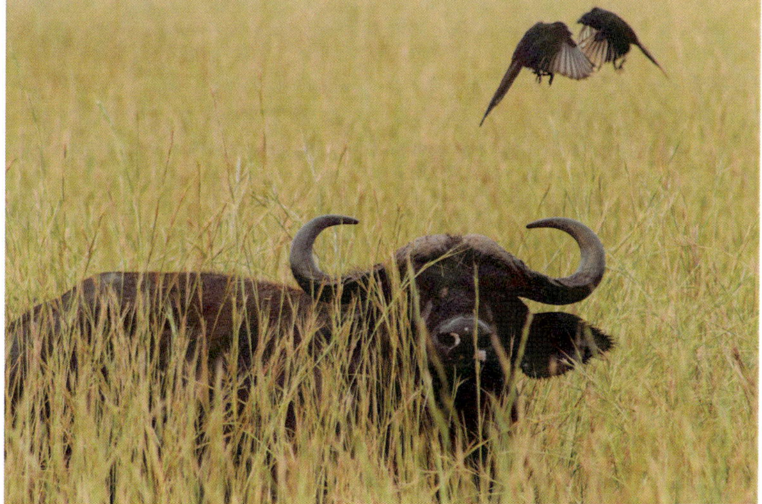

WATCHFUL AND WILD

Out of the golden grass, a buffalo rises—steady, alert, unshaken. Its gaze cuts through the savanna as birds lift into the sky above. This is the wild in balance: grounded strength below, fleeting flight above.

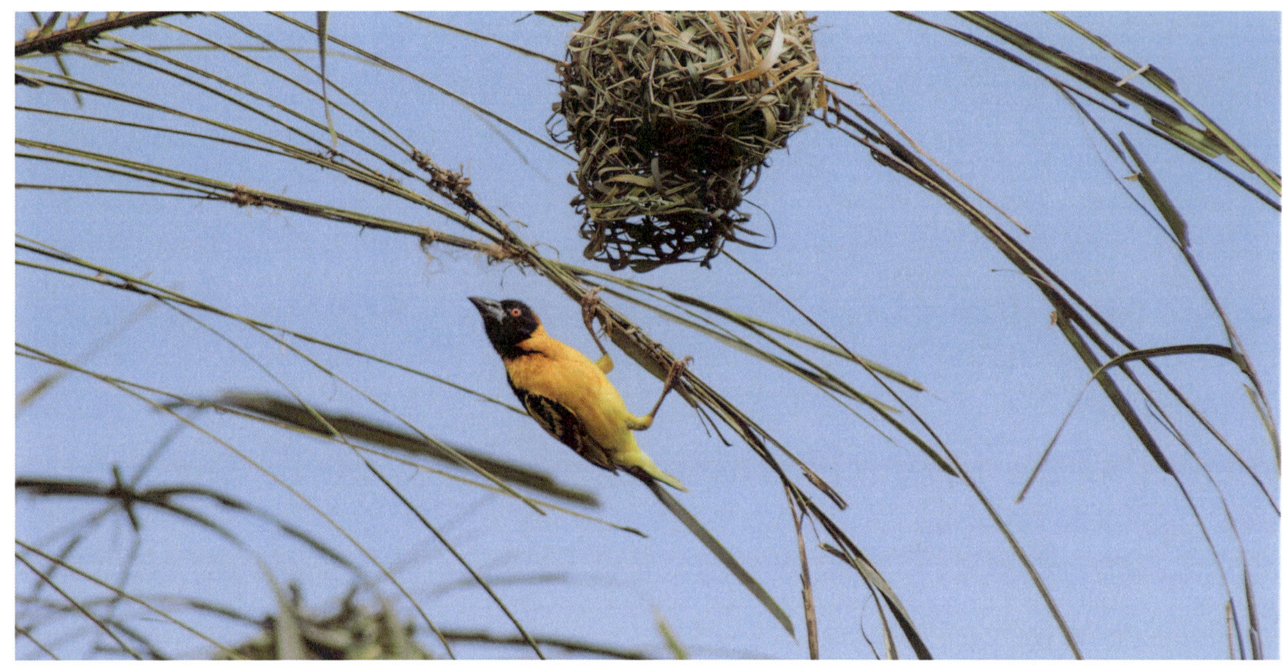

WEAVER BIRD HANGING FROM ITS NEST

Suspended midair, a weaver bird clings to its unfinished nest, a testament to nature's delicate craftsmanship. With every fiber of grass meticulously woven, this tiny architect defies the elements, creating a home that must withstand wind, rain, and predators. In the dance between fragility and determination, life perseveres.

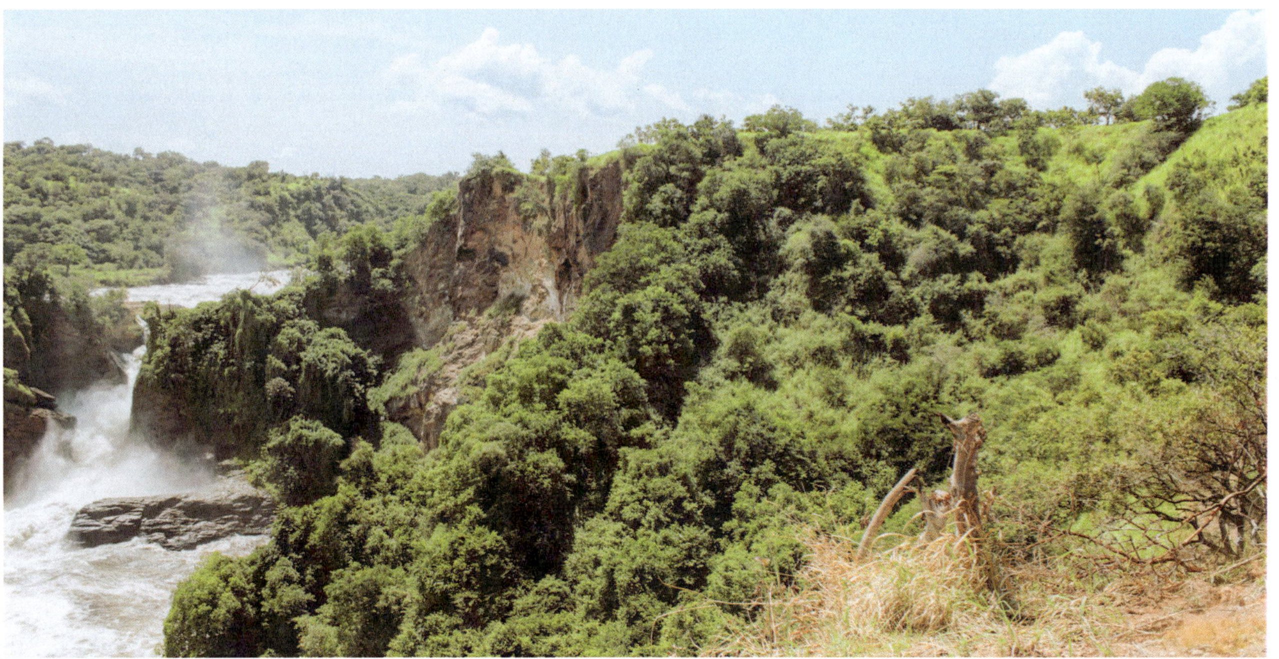

THE NILE'S UNYIELDING FORCE

Rushing over the cliff's edge, the Nile carves through ancient rock, relentless and powerful. Yet, amidst this raw force, delicate sprays of mist rise, catching the sunlight in shimmering defiance. Life thrives along the river's edge—birds, trees, and hidden creatures, all bound to the water's ceaseless rhythm.

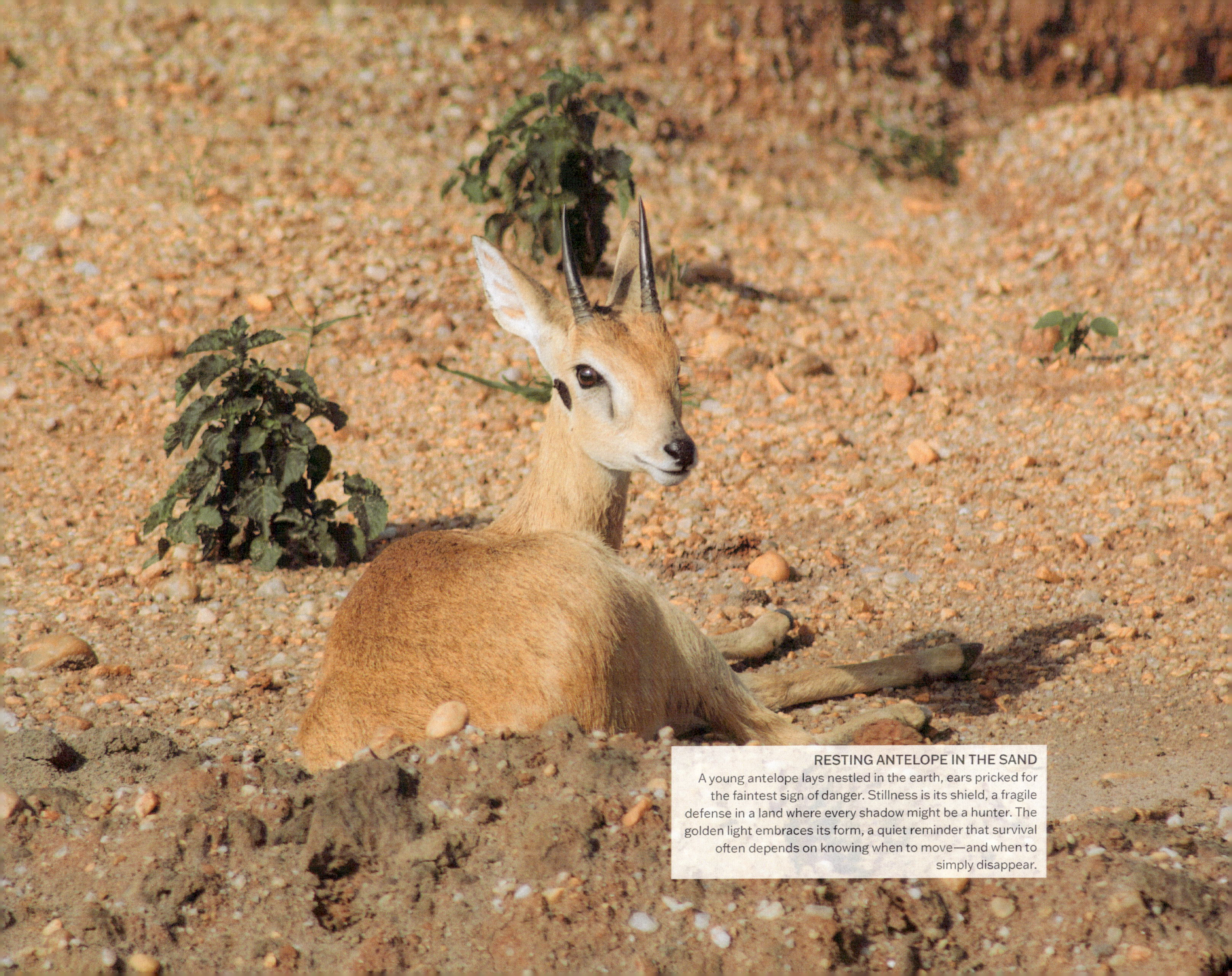

RESTING ANTELOPE IN THE SAND

A young antelope lays nestled in the earth, ears pricked for the faintest sign of danger. Stillness is its shield, a fragile defense in a land where every shadow might be a hunter. The golden light embraces its form, a quiet reminder that survival often depends on knowing when to move—and when to simply disappear.

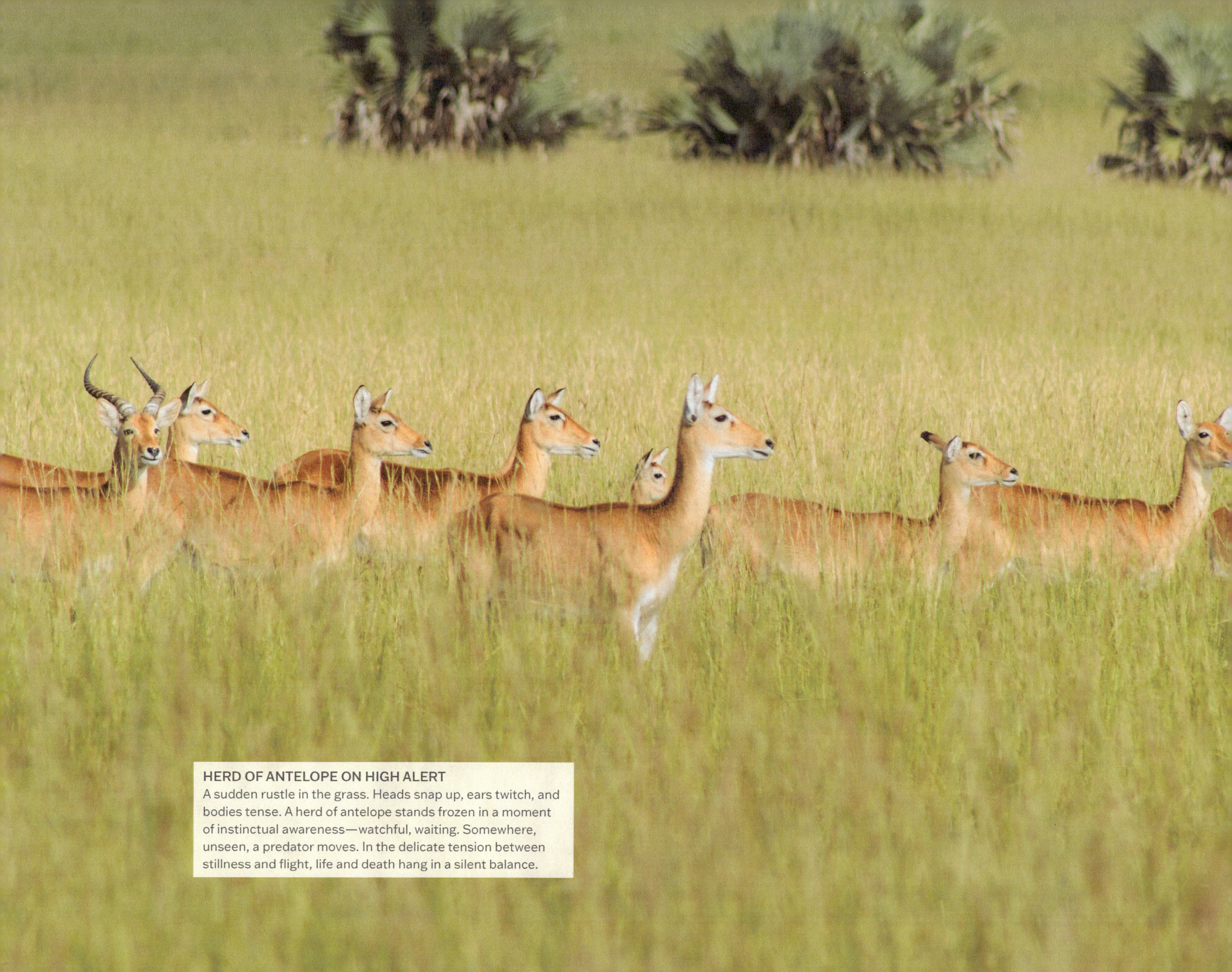

HERD OF ANTELOPE ON HIGH ALERT

A sudden rustle in the grass. Heads snap up, ears twitch, and bodies tense. A herd of antelope stands frozen in a moment of instinctual awareness—watchful, waiting. Somewhere, unseen, a predator moves. In the delicate tension between stillness and flight, life and death hang in a silent balance.

GIRAFFE IN FULL STRIDE

Graceful yet commanding, the giraffe moves across the open plains, a giant in a world where speed can mean survival. Every step is a calculated effort—stride too slow, and vulnerability becomes fatal. Yet in its towering presence, there is an elegance, a resilience carried in its rhythmic gait.

THE STALKING JACKAL

Eyes locked, muscles taut, the jackal moves with a hunter's precision. Every step is a whisper against the earth, a silent question of opportunity. In the dance of predator and prey, patience is key. Not every hunt ends in success, but for the jackal, persistence is the difference between hunger and survival.

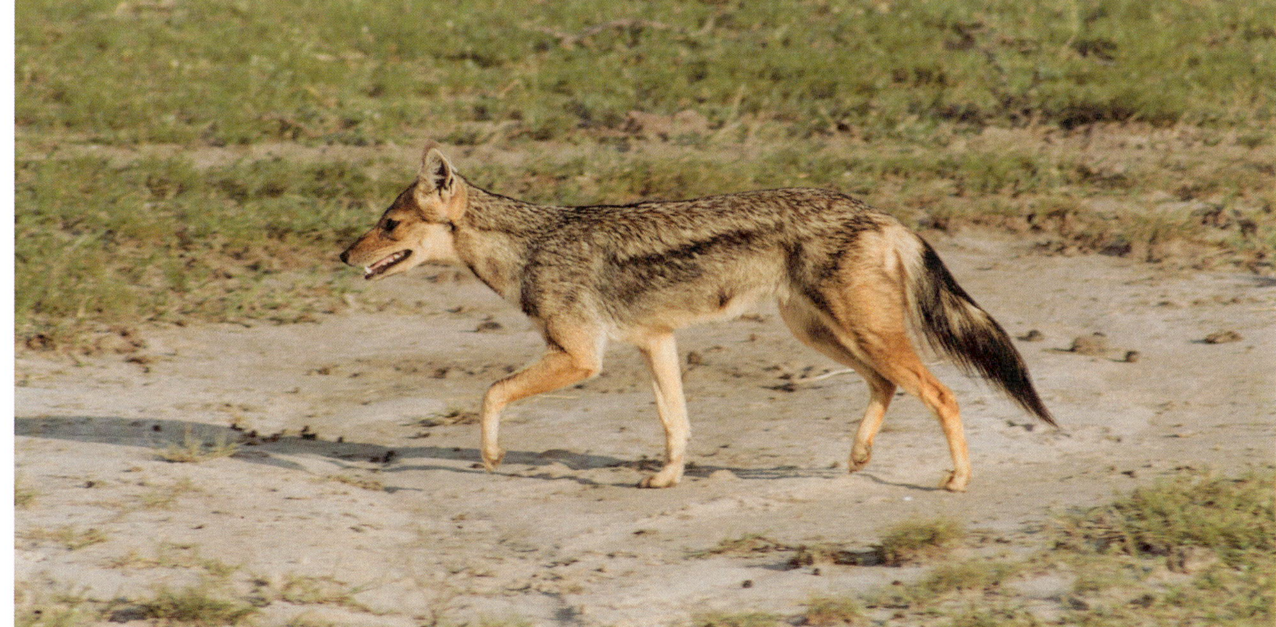

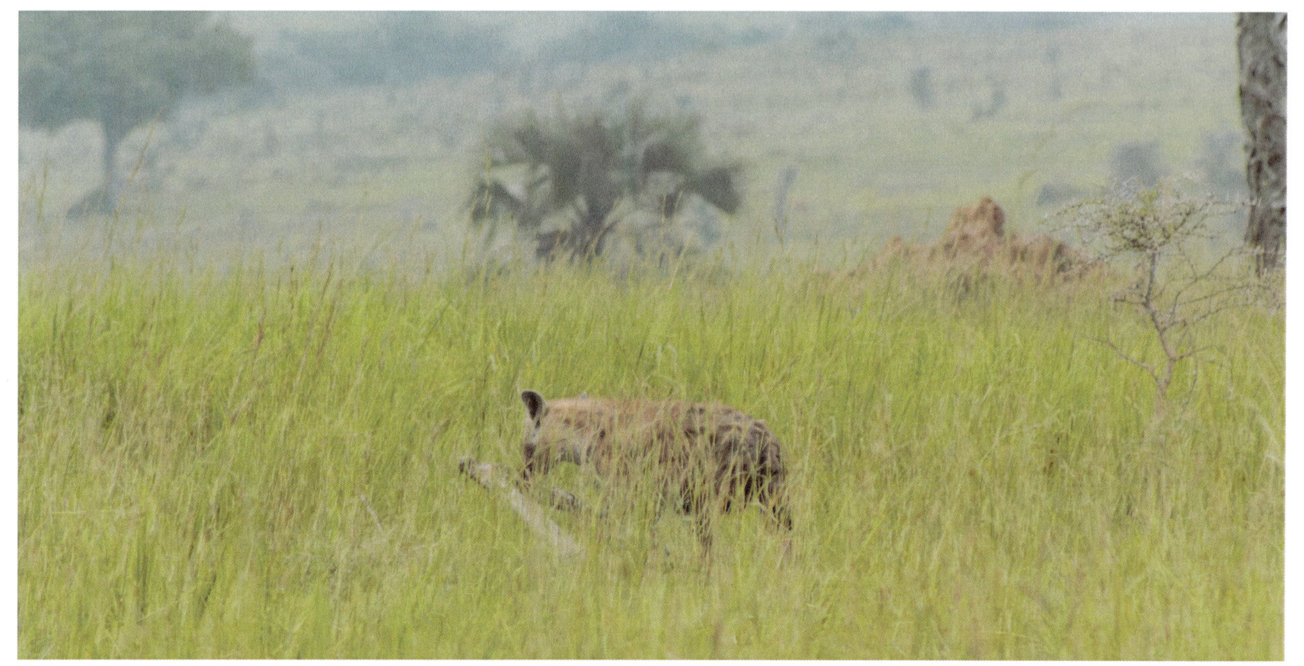

THE LONE HYENA IN THE GRASSLANDS

A solitary hyena prowls the savanna, its presence both ominous and misunderstood. Often seen as nature's scavenger, the hyena is, in truth, a survivor—one that thrives in a world of uncertainty. Where others see leftovers, it sees opportunity. In the harsh realities of the wild, nothing is wasted.

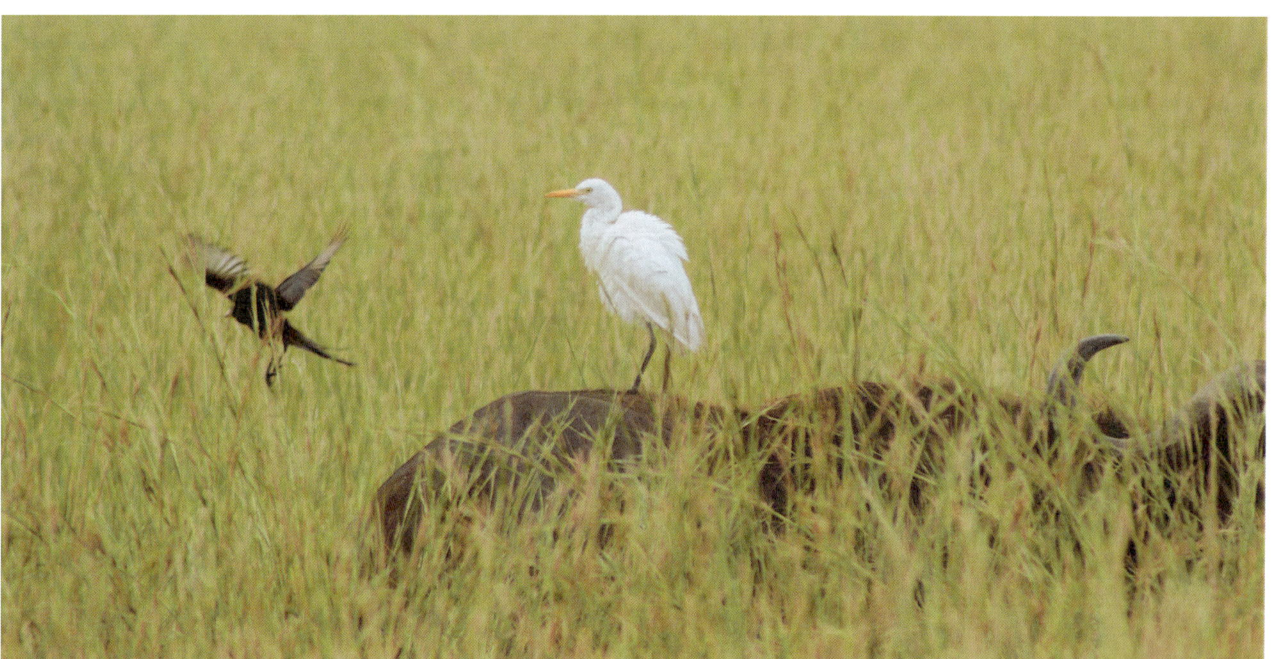

BIRD PERCHED ON BUFFALO

A white egret perches atop a buffalo's back, a silent partnership written in instinct. The buffalo's massive presence stirs up insects, a feast for the egret. In return, the bird offers a service—plucking parasites, keeping the giant free from irritation. Even in the wild, survival often depends on the quiet symbiosis between species.

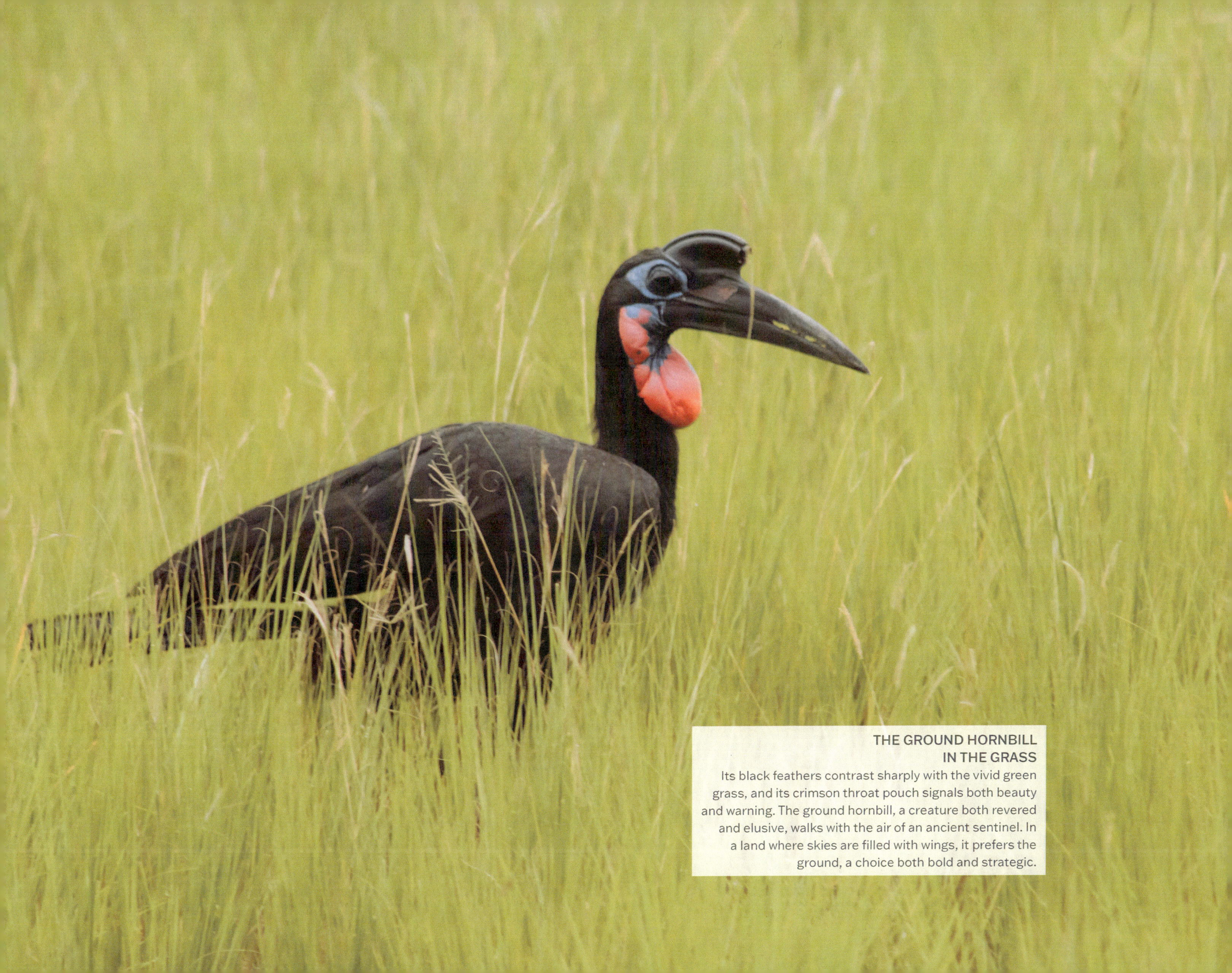

THE GROUND HORNBILL
IN THE GRASS

Its black feathers contrast sharply with the vivid green grass, and its crimson throat pouch signals both beauty and warning. The ground hornbill, a creature both revered and elusive, walks with the air of an ancient sentinel. In a land where skies are filled with wings, it prefers the ground, a choice both bold and strategic.

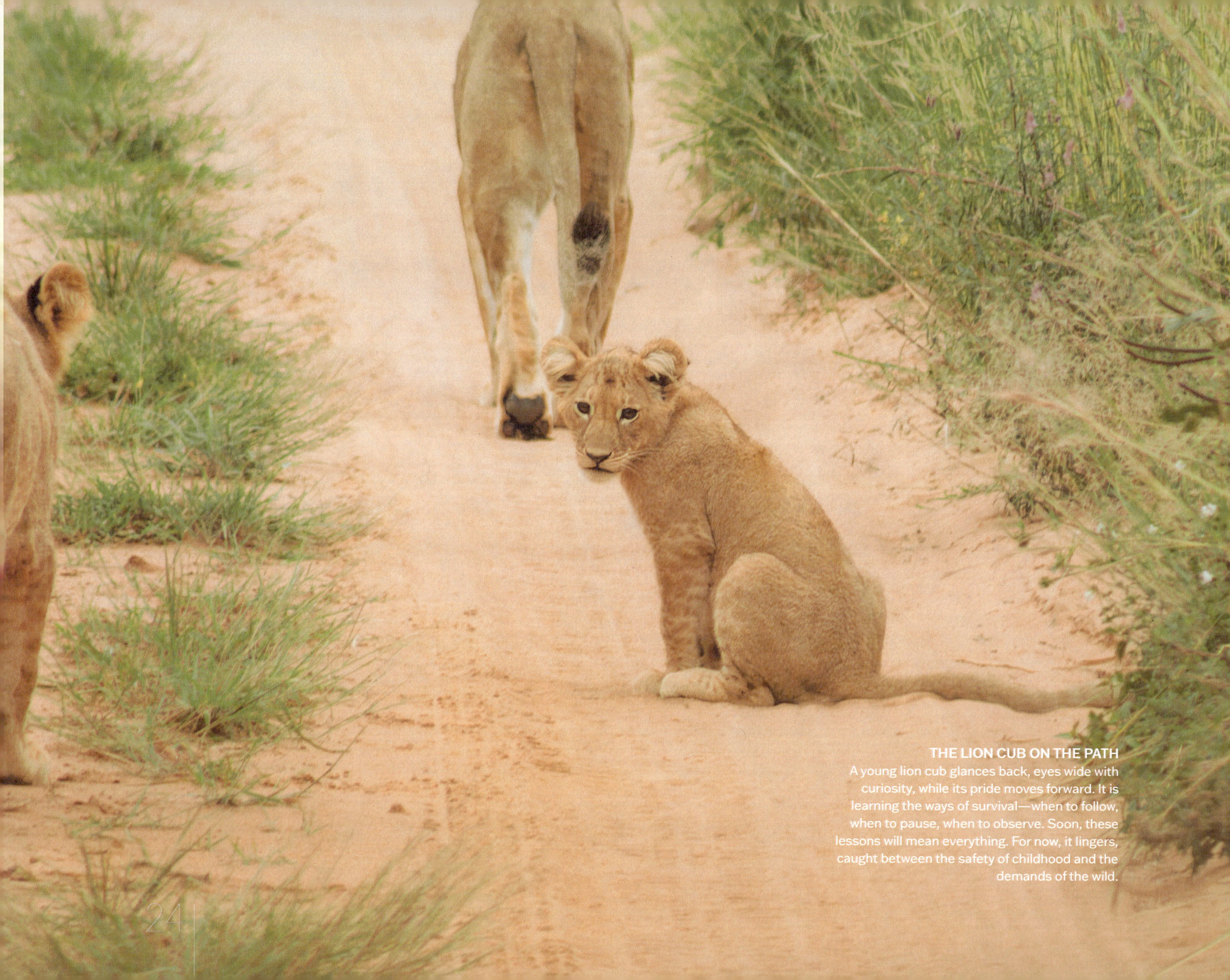

THE LION CUB ON THE PATH

A young lion cub glances back, eyes wide with curiosity, while its pride moves forward. It is learning the ways of survival—when to follow, when to pause, when to observe. Soon, these lessons will mean everything. For now, it lingers, caught between the safety of childhood and the demands of the wild.

CLIFFSIDE
BIRD NESTS

Tiny holes pepper the sheer cliffside, a vertical city of nests carved into the earth. These birds have chosen an unlikely home—one that protects them from predators but leaves them exposed to the elements. Yet, generation after generation, they return, a testament to genuis written into the rock.

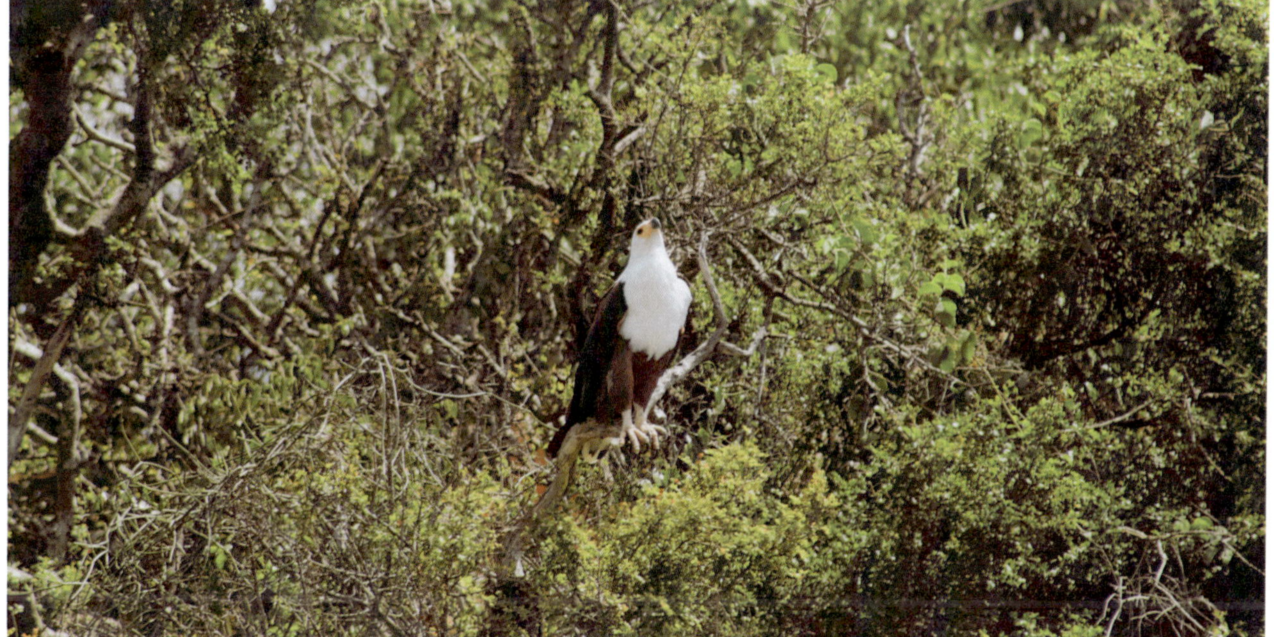

THE WATCHFUL
FISH EAGLE

Perched high above the land, the African fish eagle surveys its domain, sharp eyes scanning for movement below. It waits, patient and regal, embodying the raw power of nature. In one swift dive, it will strike, a reminder that in the wild, the strongest are not always the fastest—but the most precise.

Nature's persistence is a delicate balance: unyielding yet vulnerable, brutal yet beautiful. Every creature, from the soaring eagle to the watchful jackal, fights to survive, echoing the endurance of the land itself.

But strength is not just found in the wild. It thrives in the hands of Uganda's people: farmers, elders, and dreamers who weather hardship with unwavering determination. As we leave the rhythms of nature, we step into the stories of those who shape the land, carrying its spirit forward.

In the next chapter, we hear their voices and the stories of perseverance, survival, and the unbreakable bond between people and the land.

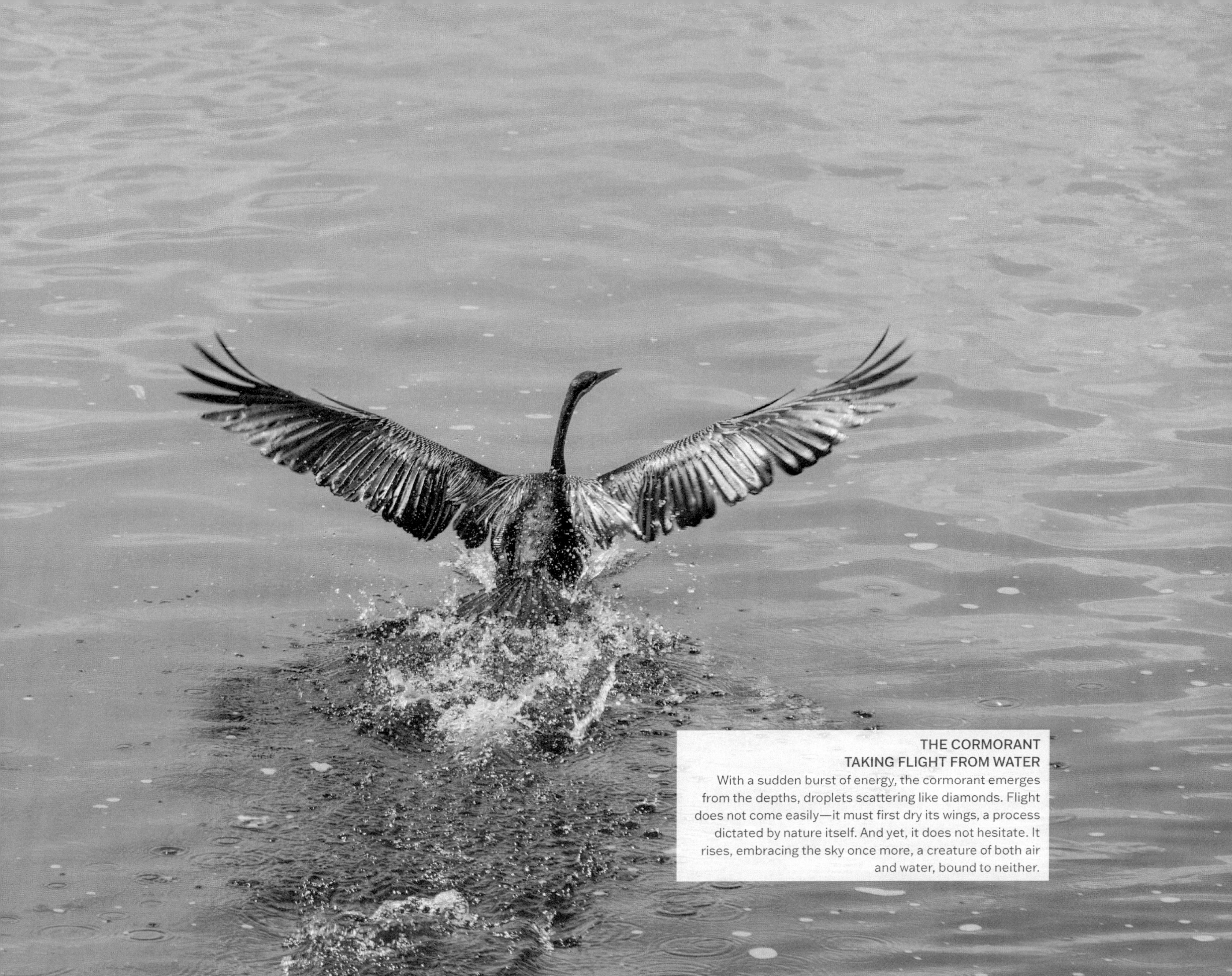

THE CORMORANT
TAKING FLIGHT FROM WATER
With a sudden burst of energy, the cormorant emerges from the depths, droplets scattering like diamonds. Flight does not come easily—it must first dry its wings, a process dictated by nature itself. And yet, it does not hesitate. It rises, embracing the sky once more, a creature of both air and water, bound to neither.

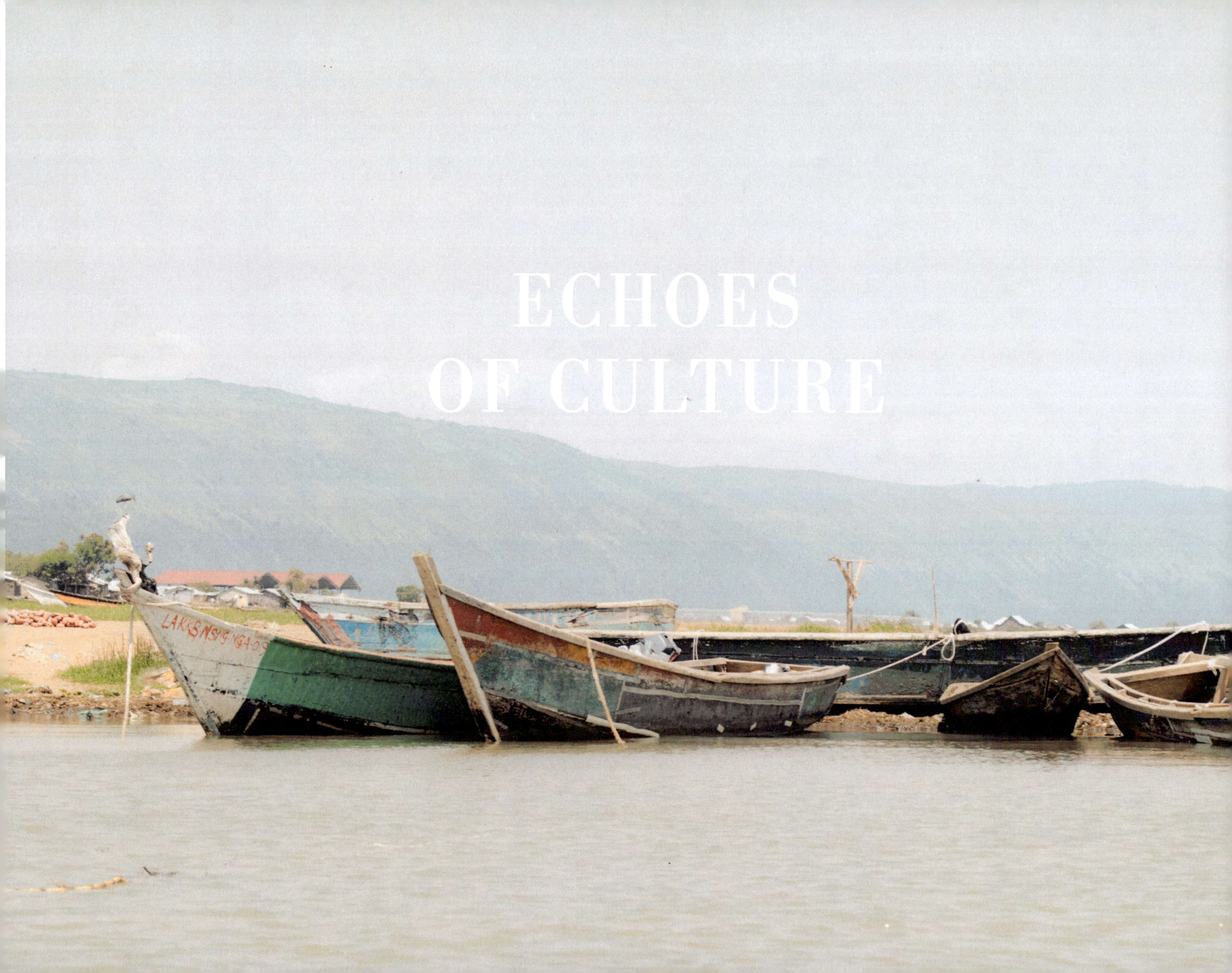
ECHOES
OF CULTURE

Across Uganda, culture is not a relic of the past, it is a living heartbeat carried in everyday life. For centuries, from the shores where Baganda ancestors first cultivated coffee along Lake Victoria for sacred ceremonies to the waters where fishing traditions pass from father to son, these practices have endured through colonial transformation, political storms, and the rebuilding of a nation. It hums in the songs children sing at play, rides the rhythm of hands shaping wood and weaving stories, and flows through the daily gathering of water that connects mothers to daughters across generations.

Here, traditions are not just remembered; they are breathed into each new day, offering both anchor and wings to a people shaped by fortitude. The same gentle techniques that sustained communities for generations still tend family gardens today. Small plots that colonial powers once tried to reshape for distant markets now thrive with ancient farming wisdom, where coffee trees planted by grandmothers still shade the homes of their grandchildren, and matoke grows alongside memories passed down through time.

In these pages, we listen for the echoes where history, hope, and identity continue to meet in the laughter of children learning traditional games, in the careful hands carving tomorrow's tools, in the evening dances that carry forward the spirits of ancestors. Through decades of change and renewal, Uganda's story unfolds as one of traditions that bend but never break, adapting to new seasons while preserving what matters most. This is Uganda's enduring spirit: vibrant in song, rooted in community, and forever rising toward tomorrow.

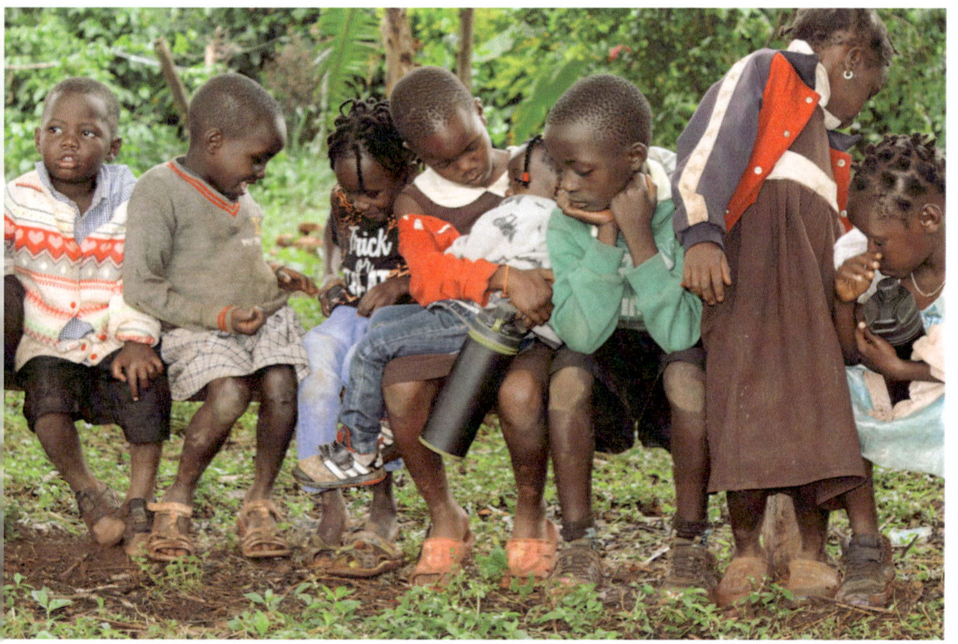

In Uganda, children grow up in a culture of shared care and quiet dignity. Here, a young orphan from Saviour Junior School gently cradles Cleofash's sleepy daughter, holding my water bottle in her other hand. There are no lines drawn between "mine" and "yours"—only community. Laughter, kindness, and connection flow naturally among them, a reflection of the values deeply rooted in Ugandan life.

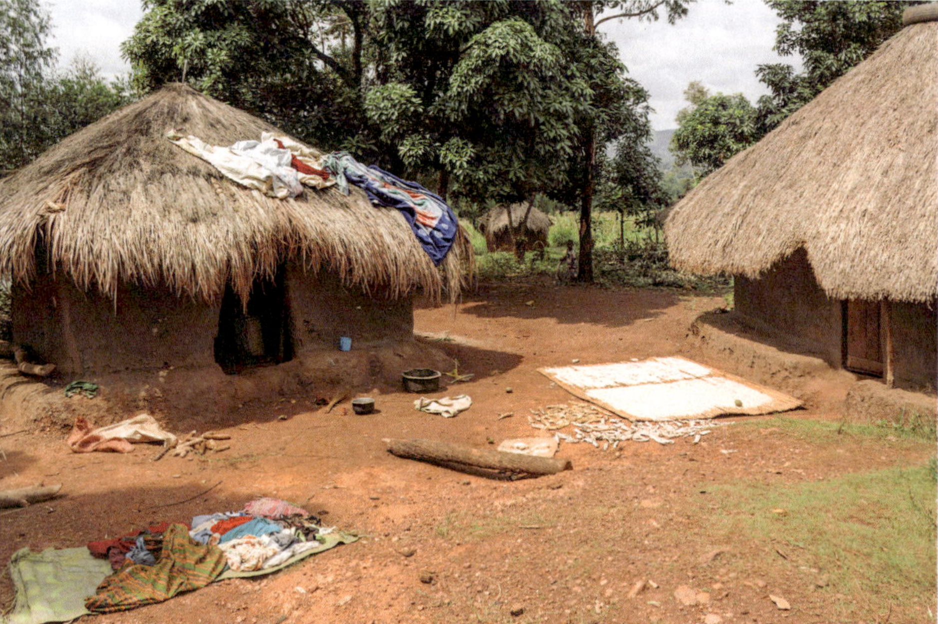

A glimpse into daily life in a rural Ugandan village. Traditional thatched-roof homes stand amid the red earth, where clothes are sun-dried on woven mats and cassava is spread out to dry beside the home. Life here flows with the rhythm of nature—resourceful, intentional, and deeply rooted in community and land.

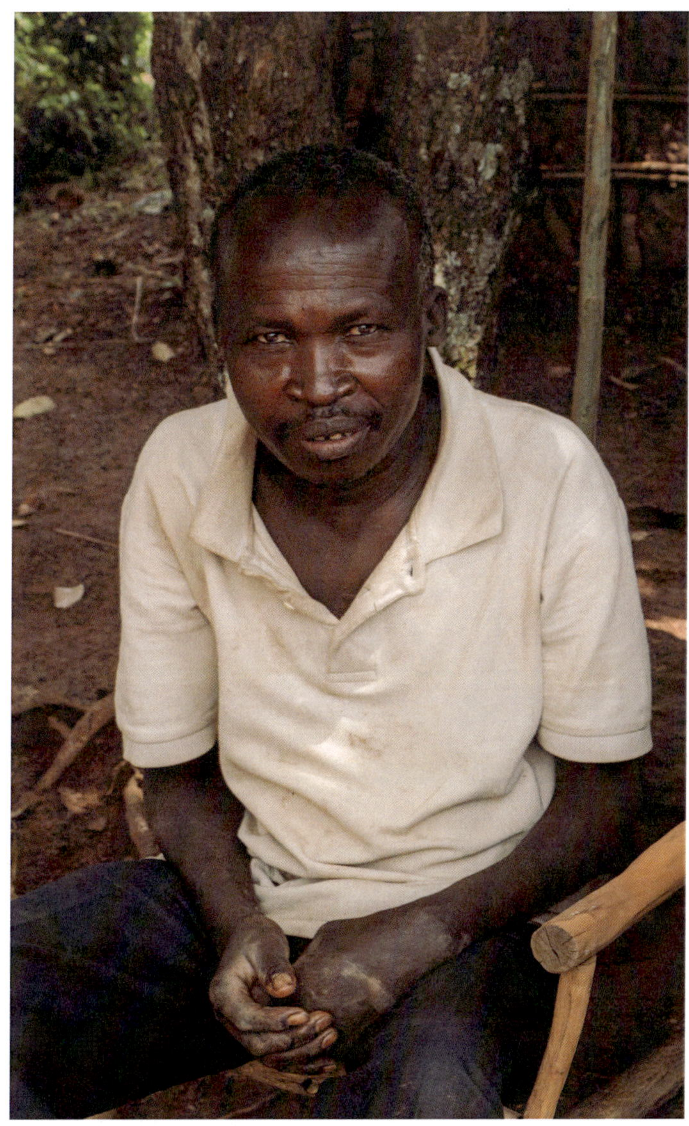 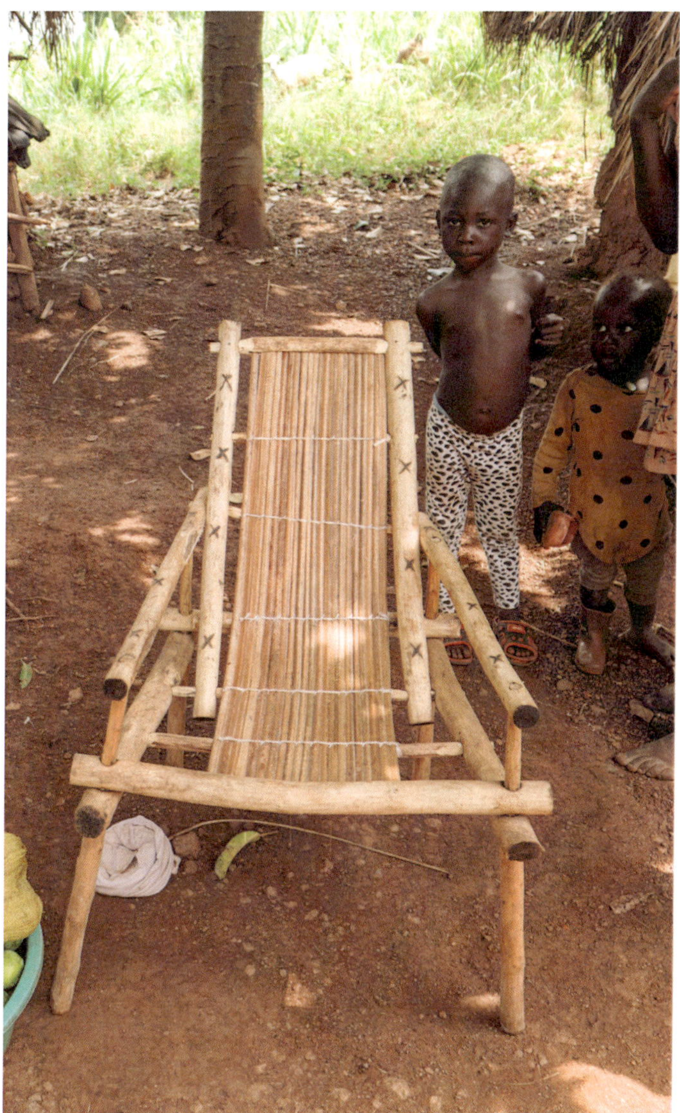

In many Ugandan communities, craftsmanship is more than skill—it's legacy. Artisans like those in Kisaba-ho village carve chairs, stools, and tools from locally sourced wood, passing techniques down through generations. These handcrafted goods often journey from rural hands to urban markets, such as Masindi town, where they're sold to support families and preserve cultural identity. Each piece tells a story—not just of utility, but of heritage, ingenuity, and pride.

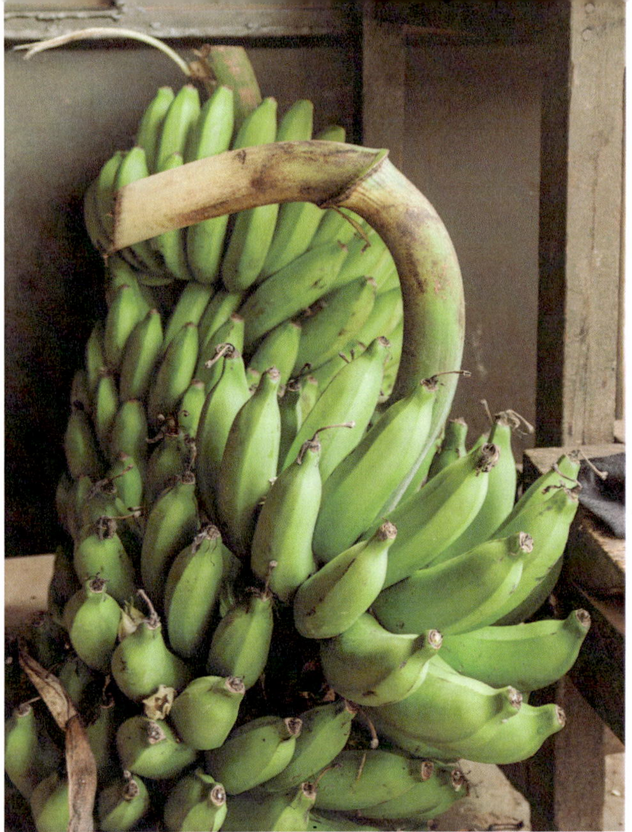

A bundle of matooke—green cooking bananas, a Ugandan staple—rests against a wooden bench. More than food, matooke is culture: a dish shared at gatherings, a symbol of hospitality, and a taste of home passed through generations.

Goldenberry jam, handcrafted by Agri Planet Africa, is more than a sweet spread—it's a reflection of Uganda's deep-rooted connection to the land, tradition, and community. Made from locally grown gooseberries, this preserve blends ancestral knowledge with modern sustainability, turning native fruits into nourishment and opportunity.

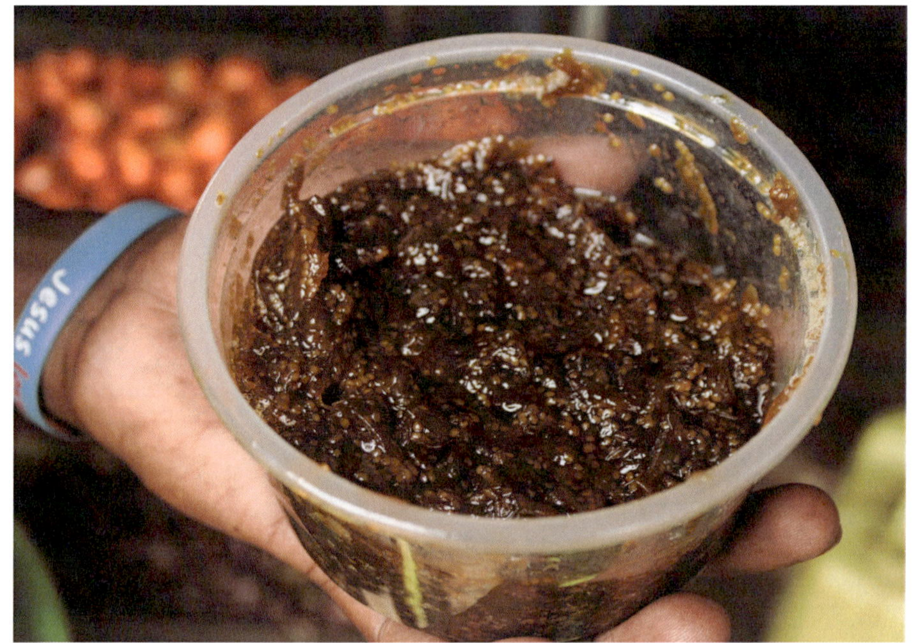

At the Nkundwa Nile View Lodge, culture came alive by firelight. Local villagers, clad in vibrant dress, filled the air with the rhythms of traditional instruments and spirited dances—an unforgettable gift on our final night. More than entertainment, their performance was a living expression of Uganda's heritage, preserved and shared through generations. The lodge plays a vital role in uplifting the community while safeguarding its cultural soul.

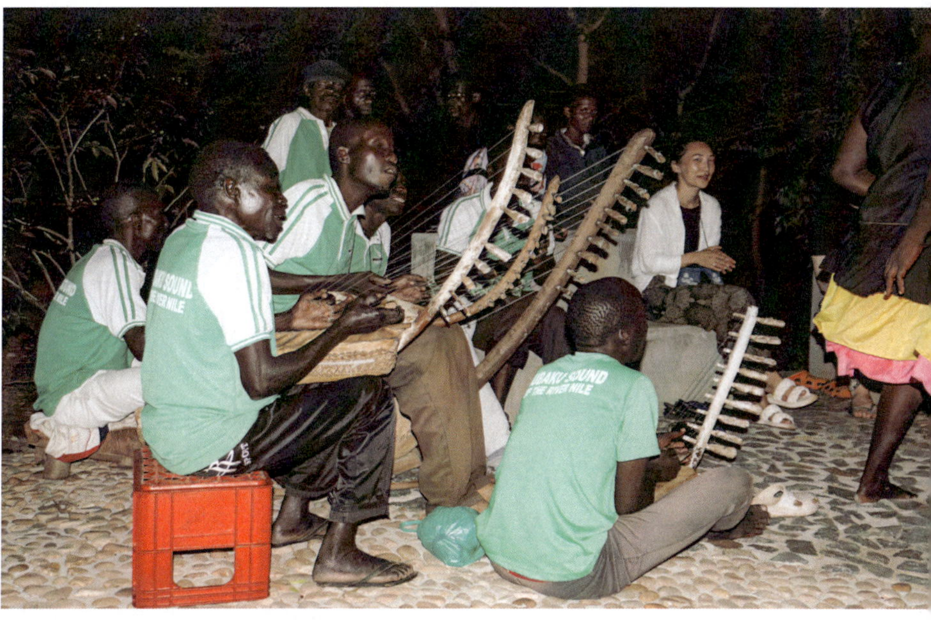

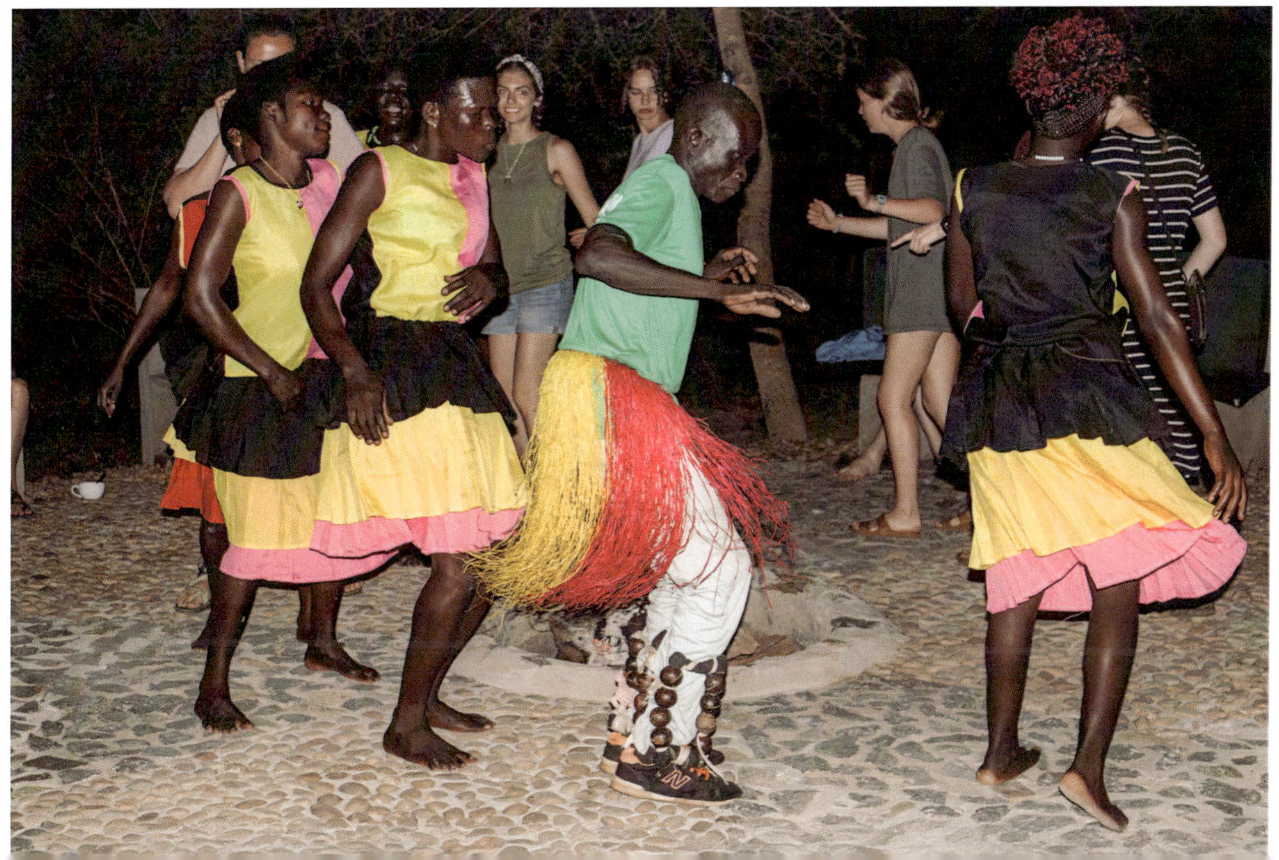

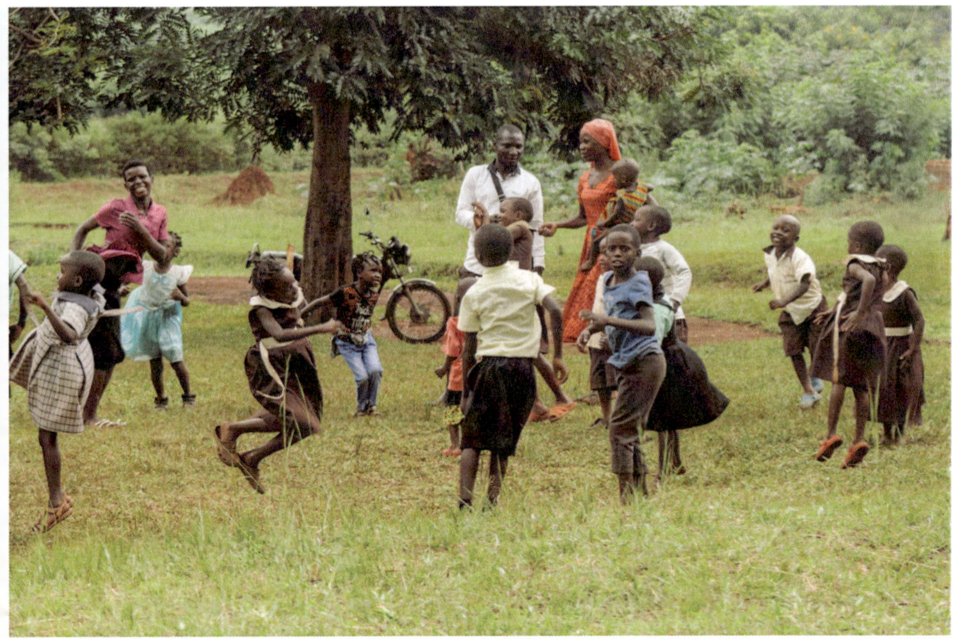

At Saviour Junior School, lessons unfold in rhythm and joy. Children learn traditional songs like "Fire on the Mountain, Run Run Run," melodies that carry safety, heritage, and the wisdom of generations. Behind them, a boda-boda leans against a tree, not just a vehicle, but a symbol of movement, income, and connection. With the care of devoted teachers and the school's director, this moment captures Uganda's living legacy where culture, community, and spirit dance together.

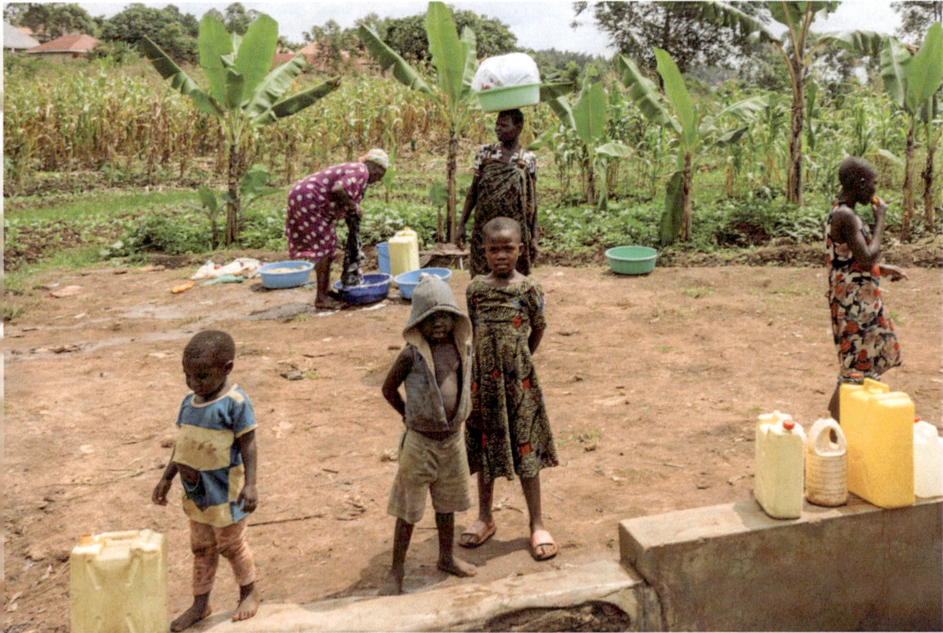

In the village of Kisabaho, nestled within Masindi municipality's Kigulya Division, the water source becomes a daily gathering place. Here, children and women shoulder the vital task of fetching clean water for cooking, cleaning, and drinking: a tradition woven into the rhythm of rural life. With banana groves behind them and jerry cans at their feet, they carry more than water: they carry the enduring strength of their community.

Traditions are not just remembered;
they are breathed into each new day

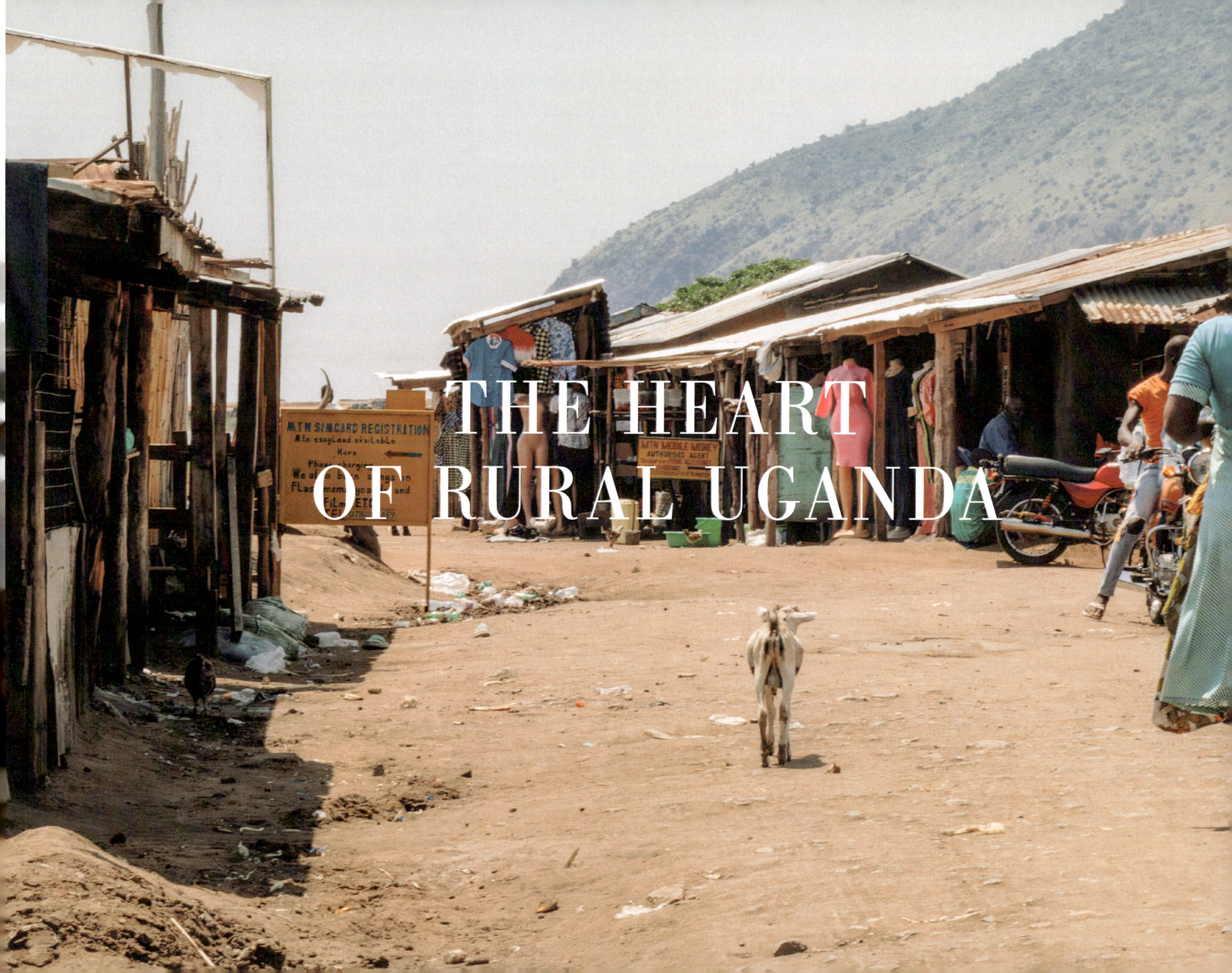
THE HEART
OF RURAL UGANDA

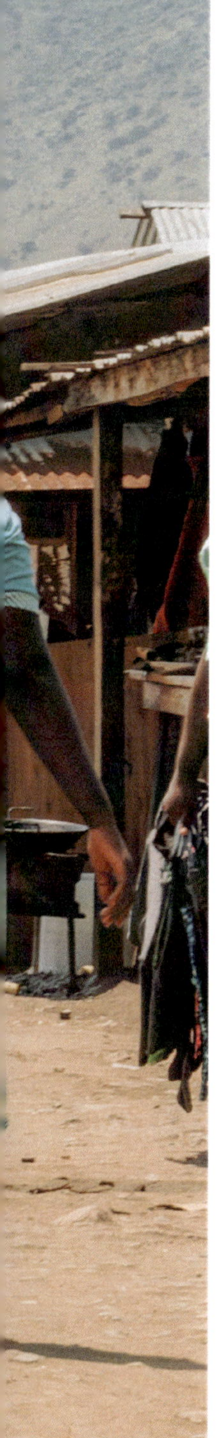

Beyond Uganda's bustling towns and wild preserves lies another kind of beauty: the quiet, enduring spirit of its rural heartlands.

Here, life moves with the rhythm of the land. Fishermen haul their nets at dawn along the shores of Lake Albert, while farmers press seeds into rich, forgiving soil. In the shade of ancient trees, generations gather: mothers nursing babies, children laughing as goats dart through the fields, elders sharing stories older than memory itself.

Across these scattered communities (Kikuube, Masindi, Miirya, Lake Albert, and beyond) we found a deeper kind of strength. Not the loud, triumphant kind, but the quiet determination stitched into red clay roads, weathered boats, and sun-warmed hands. It's in the laughter that arises after long days of work, in the children's eager smiles, in the pride woven through each small market and quiet homestead.

This chapter is not a portrait of one place, but a tapestry of many, each thread carrying its own story of perseverance, humility, and hope.

As you walk these pages, may you feel the warmth of the sun on your shoulders, the dust of the path beneath your feet, and breathe in the rich earthen scent that rises after rain mingled with wood smoke from evening fires, the green sweetness of growing things, and the distant warmth of spices simmering in clay pots. May you sense the strength of communities who live each day grounded in the richest kind of wealth: connection, tradition, and unbreakable spirit.

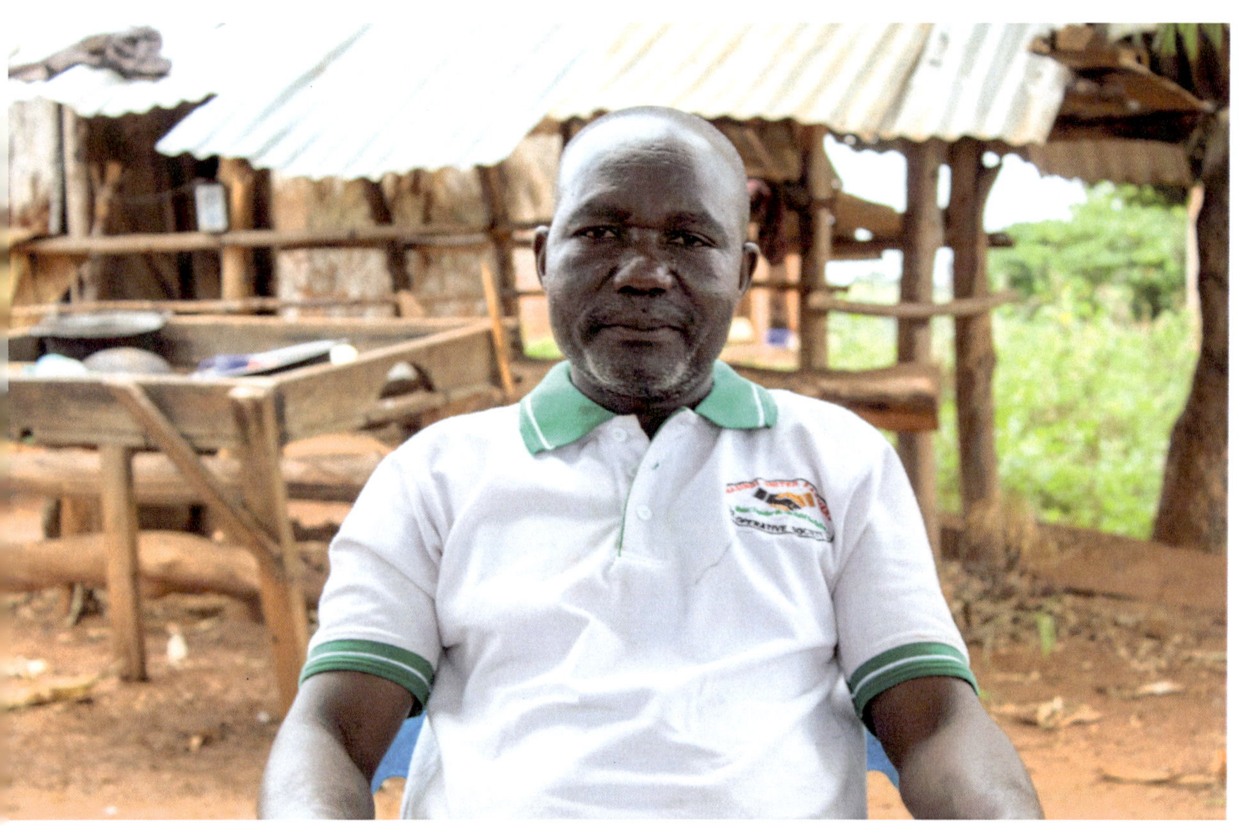

While walking from our golden berry fields toward the Agri-Planet Grocers shop in Masindi, our team passed through an indigenous village and met a local councilman. His calm, steady presence reflected the deep roots he had in his community. He was very welcoming and calm, exuding the quiet wisdom that drew me in. As we spoke, he shared some of the challenges the community faces, particularly around teenagers becoming pregnant early and missing out on school if they could even afford it. His commitment to his community was evident: he spoke with a sense of responsibility and care, determined to do what he could for everyone. When he asked how many children I had, I pointed to my daughter, Lena, and said, "Just one." He laughed heartily, thinking I was joking. I wasn't. He proudly shared he had 17 children, a reflection of the different rhythms of life here.

This brief but meaningful exchange highlighted the warmth and generosity of the community. His portrait captures the leadership and tradition that sustain indigenous life, reminding me of the beauty found in simple, heartfelt conversations.

A young boy from Kobusinge, Uganda stands quietly amidst the celebration of Agri Planet Africa's second Community Permaculture Resource Center, where over 110 trees had just been planted. His confident gaze and gentle spirit lingered long after he slipped his small hand into mine, a living emblem of the wonder and curiosity that runs through rural Uganda's youngest hearts.

The day was filled with laughter, the aroma of fresh vegan meals, and the sounds of children playing freely across the land they were helping to heal. In communities like Kobusinge, the act of planting trees becomes more than conservation; it becomes a covenant with the future, a promise rooted in unity, hope, and the enduring strength of the land and its people.

Through portraits like his, the spirit of rural Uganda comes alive: farmers tending crops with calloused hands, children weaving dreams in the dust, and elders passing down wisdom like seeds, all stitched together by the quiet, unbreakable threads of connection and continuity.

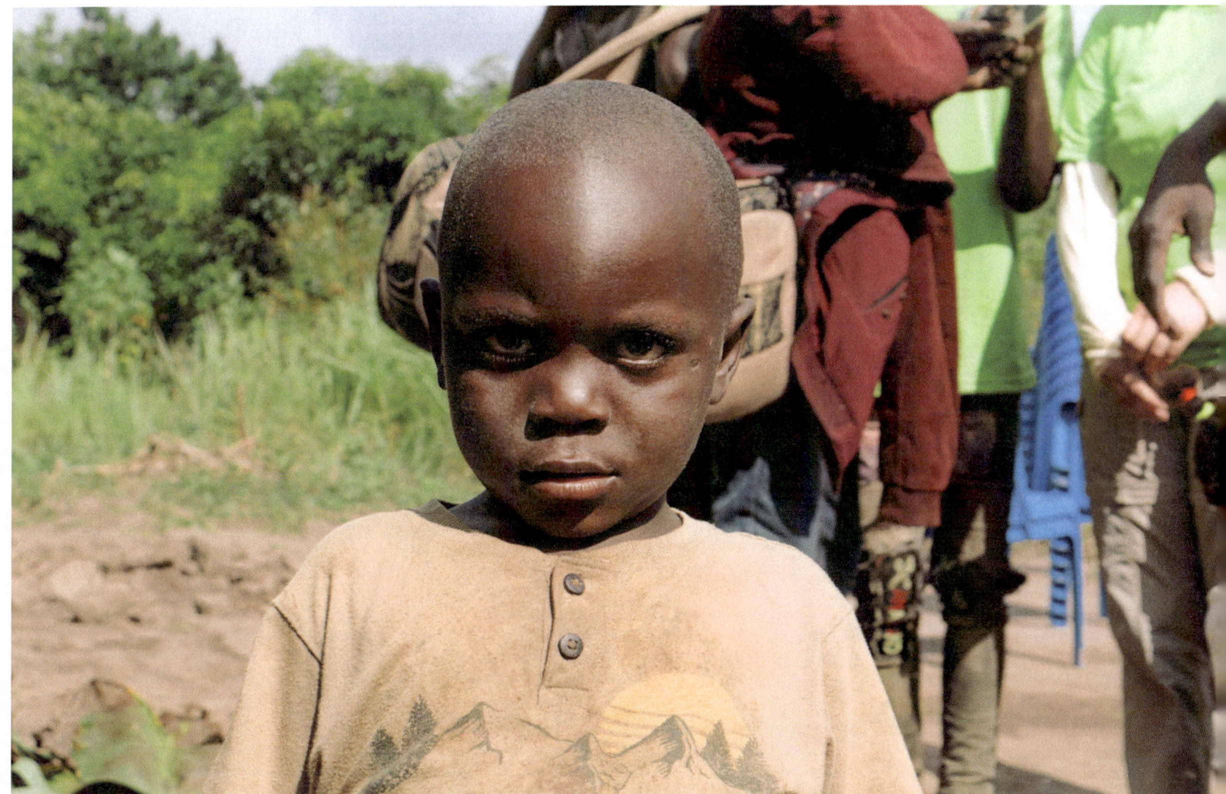

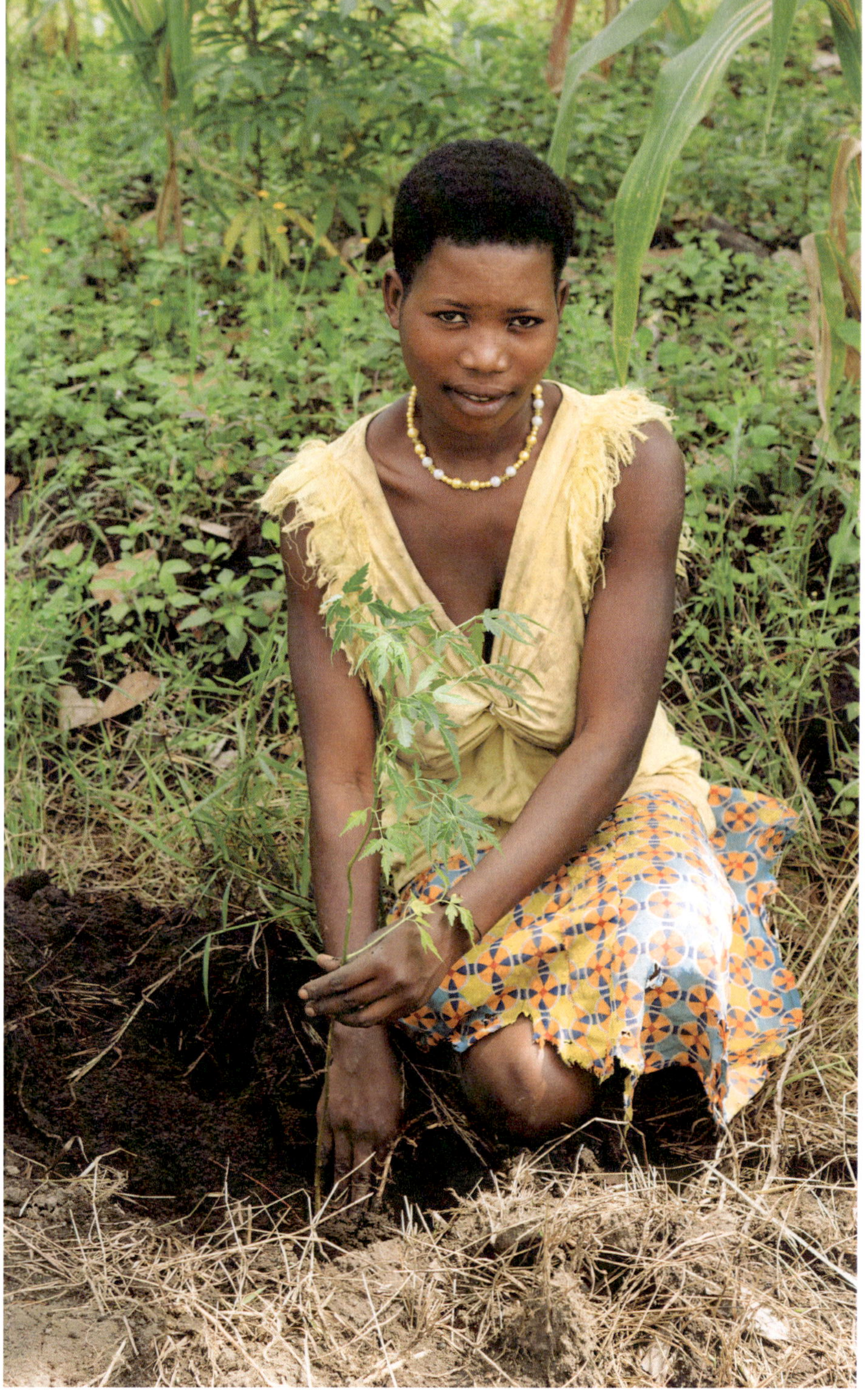

Beneath the sweltering sun of Kobusinge, a young woman plants a tree with quiet determination, her vibrant yellow dress shining like a beacon against the rich soil. Each planted sapling carries more than roots; it carries the weight of dreams, a living testament to hope and renewal.

Around her, neighbors gather, laughing and sharing stories as they work side by side, stitching their future into the land with every handful of earth. Her unwavering spirit and the unity of her community reveal a deeper truth: strength is not built in isolation but is cultivated in shared moments, small acts, and the promise of a greener tomorrow.

At the Bugoma landing site on Lake Albert, near the Congo border, life moves to the timeless rhythm of water and wind. Here, fishing transcends livelihood to become a legacy. With practiced hands and patient strength, fishermen clean their fresh catch along the lakeshore, the sun casting sharp reflections across the water and the scent of fish hanging in the air like a memory.

The dry, challenging soil of the region leaves little room for farming, making the lake not only a source of sustenance but a lifeline. Each movement echoes the careful cut of a knife, the steady pull of a net, and the wisdom built over generations.

In the buzz of labor and the soft lapping of waves, the spirit of the community endures: resourceful, enduring, and woven into the natural rhythms of Lake Albert's wild, untamed beauty.

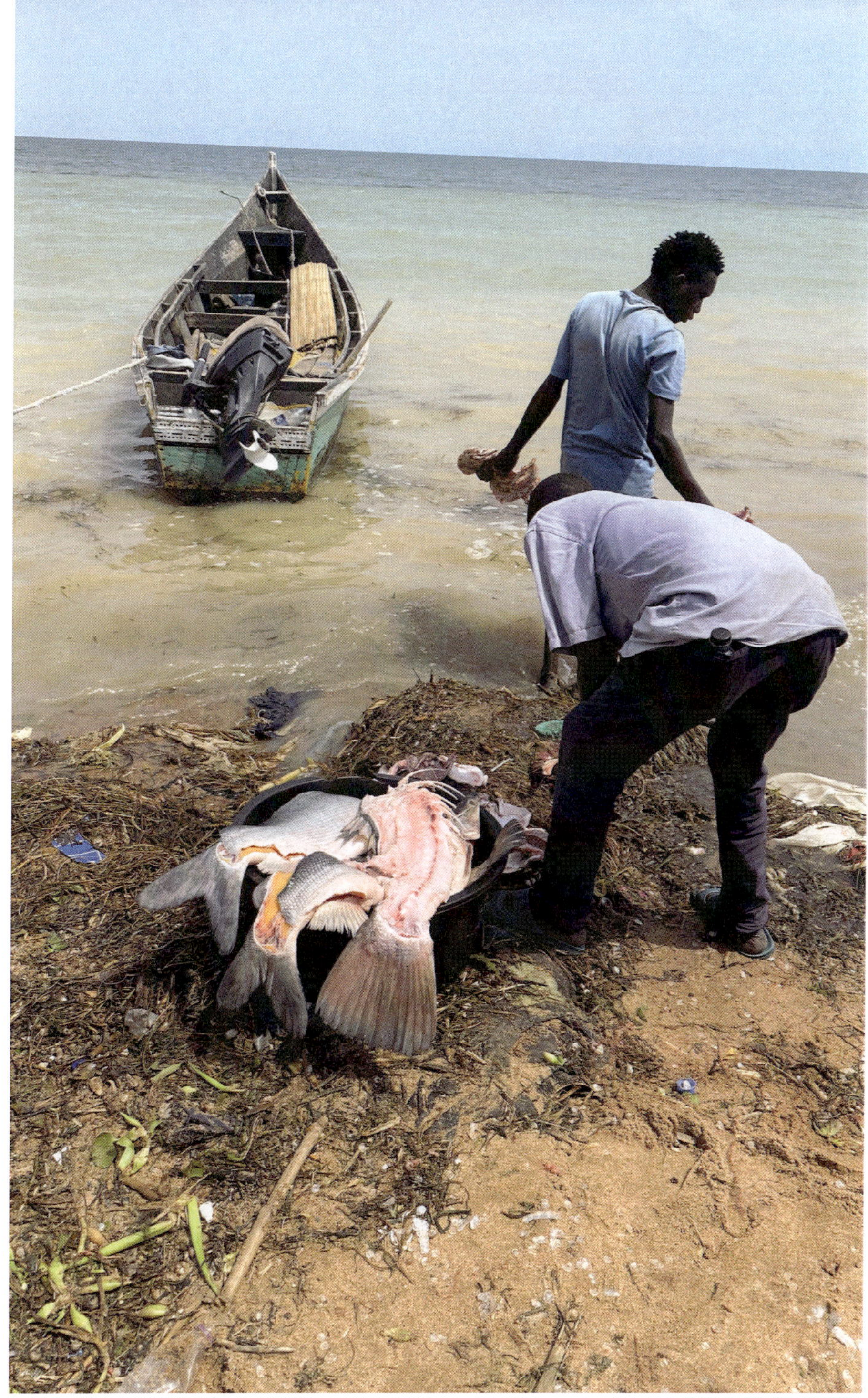

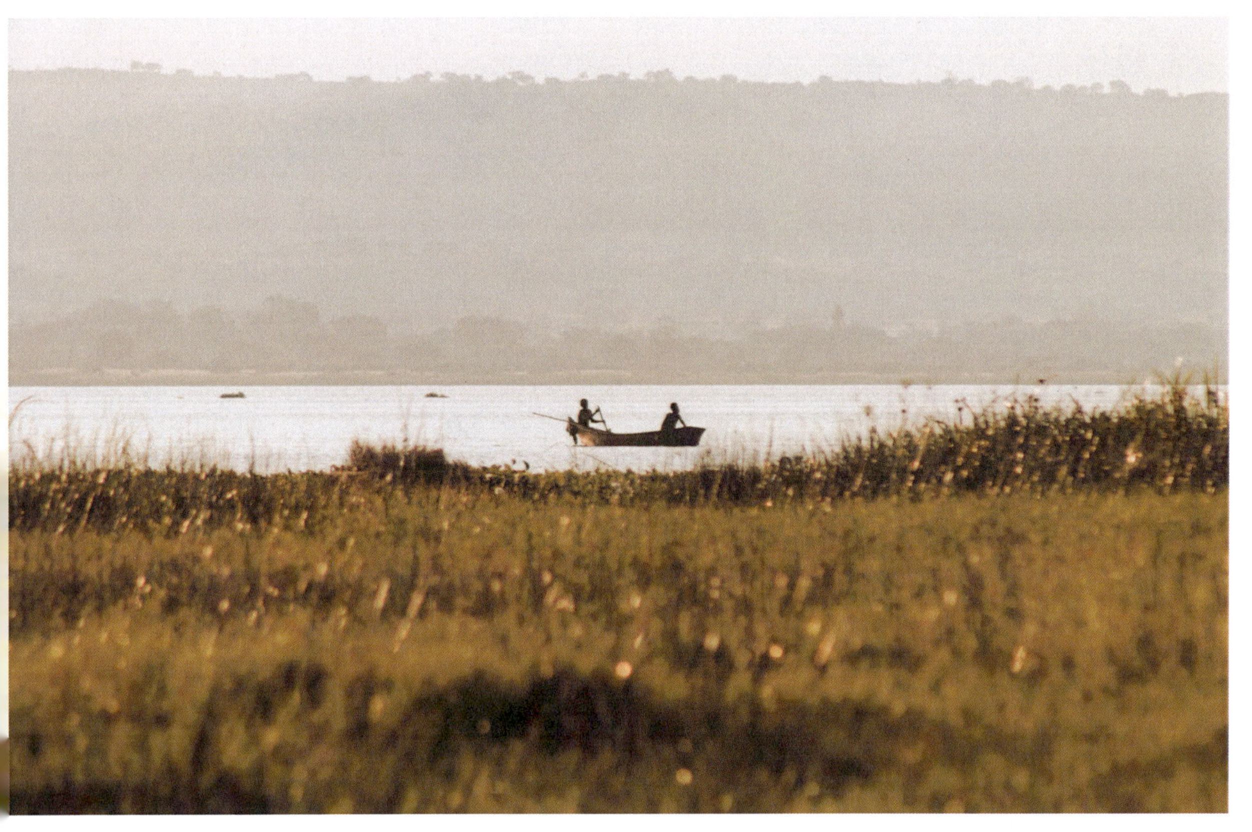

A lone boat glides across still waters, a quiet witness to the rhythms of rural life.

Here, the bond between people and nature runs deeper than memory—an inheritance passed down through hands that fish, farm, and build with quiet reverence.

Beyond the horizon, generations have lived by the wisdom of the land and water, moving with its tides, trusting its seasons.

This moment, bathed in soft light, speaks of journeys rather than destinations, of an inheritance that floats, steady and sure, across the currents of time.

Amid the tall, green maize stalks, Komujuni Allen Shanita (*Akiiki*), wife of Agri Planet Africa's CEO Ignatius and mother to Janelle, moves with quiet grace. After spending hours carefully preparing a meal for six of us—cooking over small camping-style stoves—she transitioned seamlessly to washing dishes, her vibrant red shirt and steady smile radiating warmth and generosity.

Her actions were a living portrait of hospitality woven into everyday life: offering the best of what she had, with patience, joy, and grace. In moments like these, the true spirit of community revealed itself—not in abundance of resources, but in abundance of heart. Strength here is not declared, it is quietly lived, passed down through hands and hearts alike.

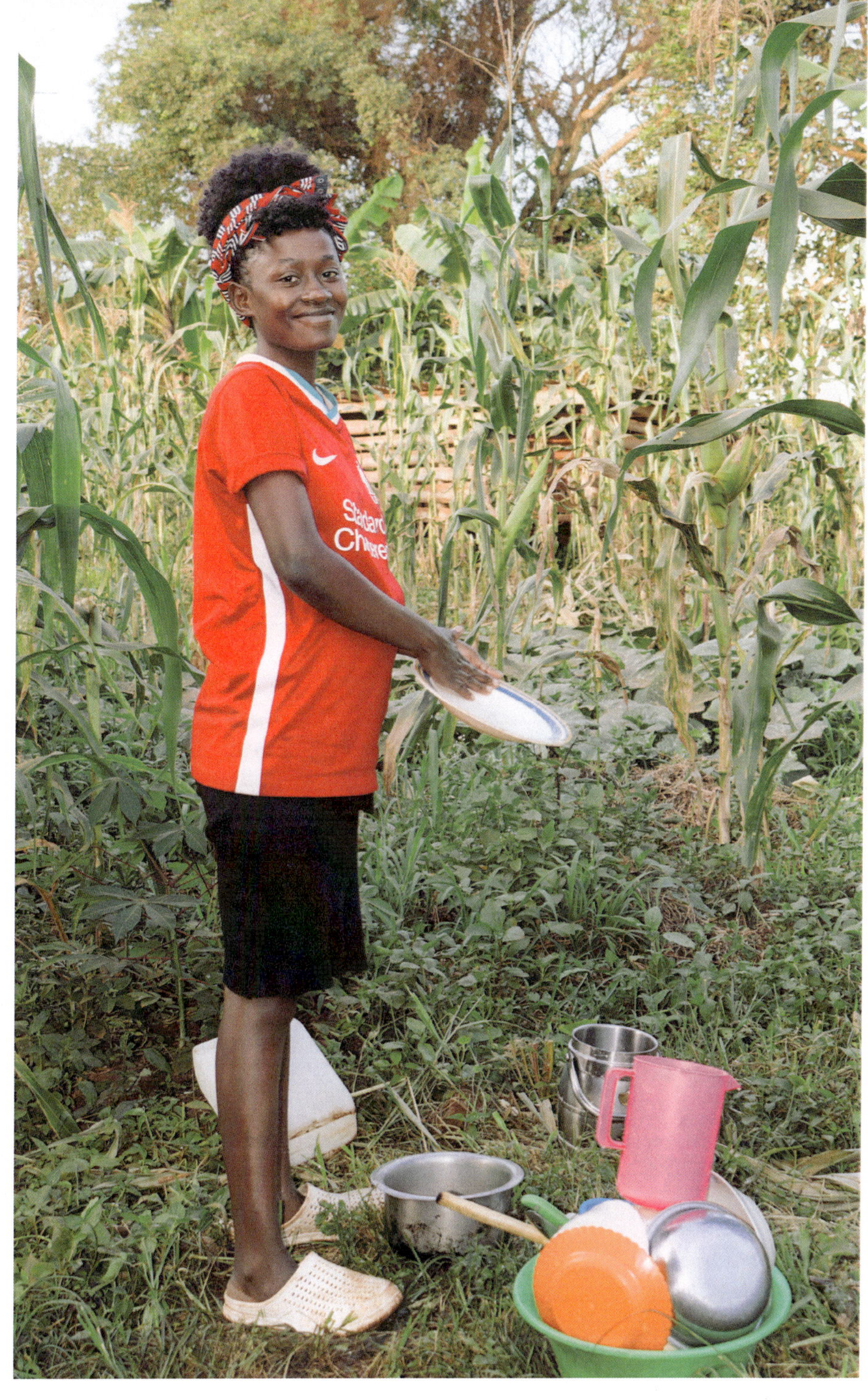

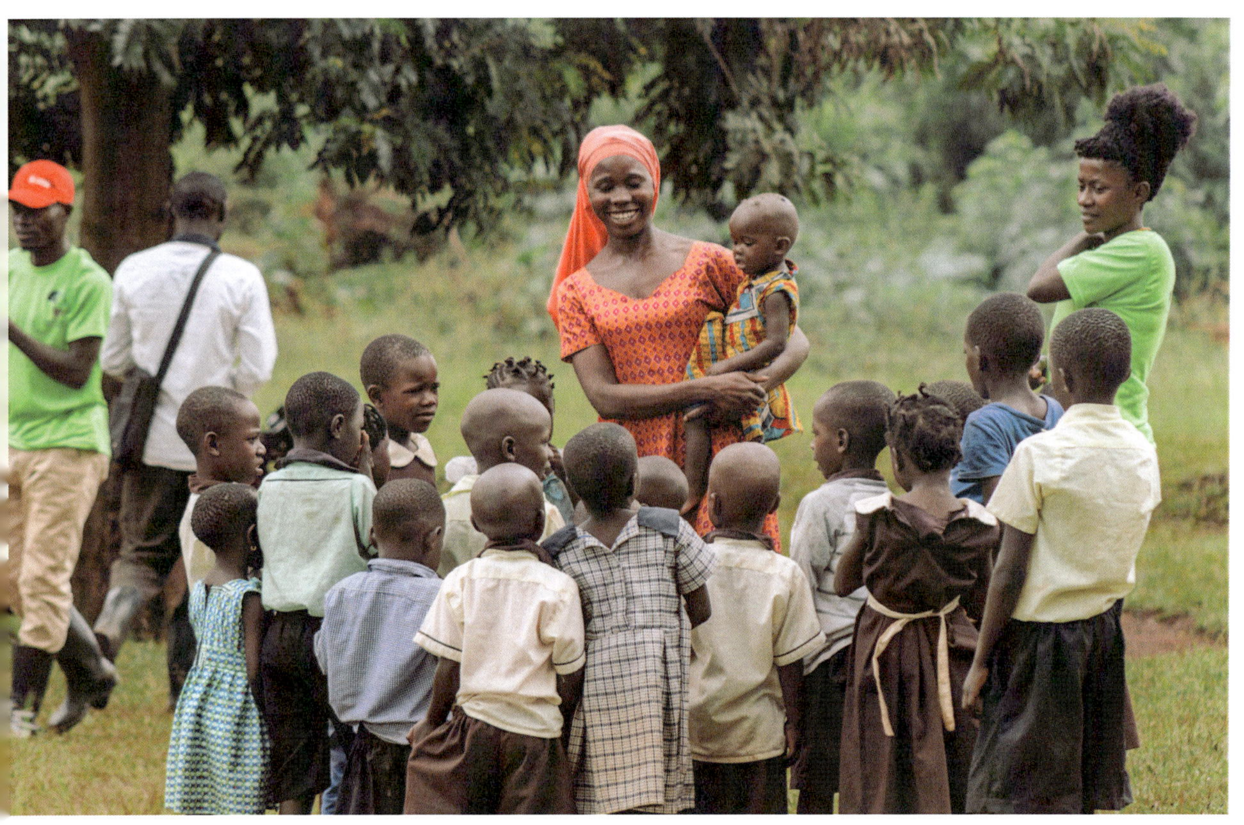

A teacher at Saviour Junior School stands with quiet strength among her students, a young child resting peacefully in her arms. Her presence is steady, her smile soft—offering more than instruction: offering safety.

The children gather in a wide circle, their backs turned as they listen, surrounded by the tender hush of a schoolyard that has known both struggle and hope.

There are no blackboards here, but the lesson is clear: learning begins in trust, and education grows strongest where it's rooted in care.

Beneath the watchful shade of towering trees, women and children sit quietly outside a village home near Masindi. One mother cradles a child on her lap while others rest close beside her, their bodies angled in comfort, their gaze soft and steady.

Behind them, a weathered home stands with quiet pride, its worn doorway holding stories of generations past. Laundry flutters nearby like whispered memories—evidence of daily life moving gently forward.

There is no spectacle here—only the deep hum of endurance. A portrait of quiet strength, stitched together by shared rhythms, shared soil, and the unspoken power of being present.

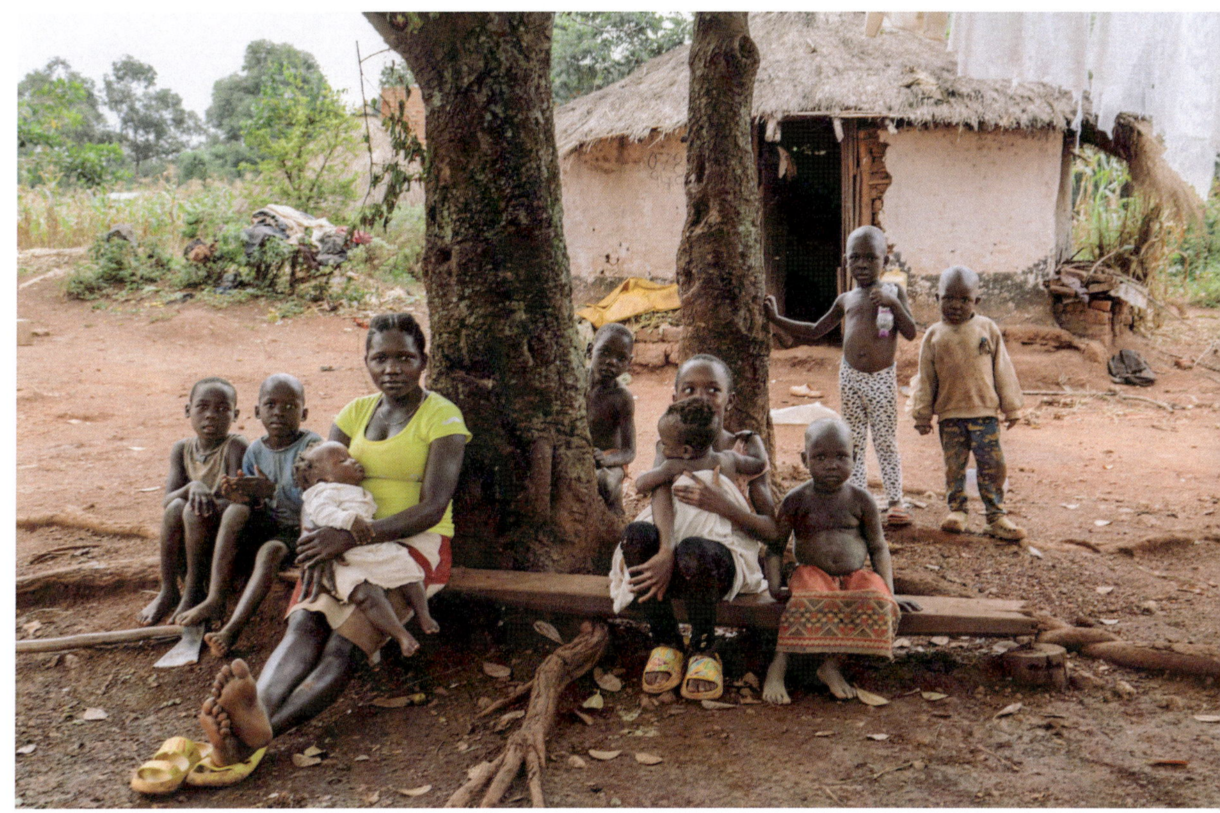

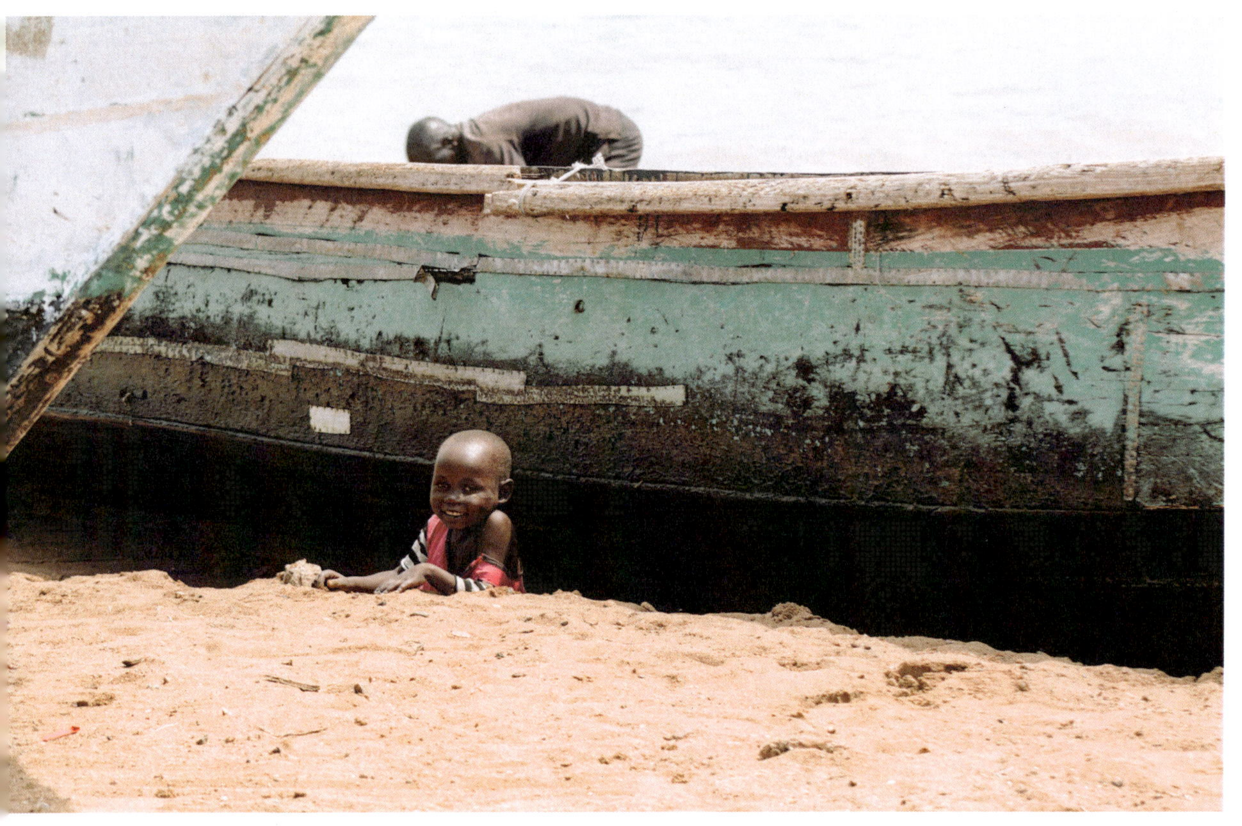

A little girl beams brightly from beneath the shade of a weathered fishing boat along the shores of Lake Albert. Her sparkling eyes and playful hands in the sand capture a moment of pure, unguarded joy.

Around her, fishermen work with practiced hands, the scent of lake water and fresh catch filling the air. The worn, peeling paint of the boat tells stories of generations who have lived by the cadence of these waters, but her laughter brings a new story of hope and joy and the enduring spirit of childhood.

Even in a place shaped by hard work and survival, moments like this remind us: joy takes root wherever hearts are open and life is embraced in all its simple, beautiful forms.

Along a dusty road winding through the Ugandan countryside, a group of children paused their journey to greet a stranger. Shy smiles danced between them—curious, playful, a little uncertain but full of light. Their laughter echoed softly against the hills, a reminder that even in the quietest corners of the world, connection can bloom without a single word. In their gaze was the spirit of rural Uganda: welcoming, vibrant, and endlessly alive.

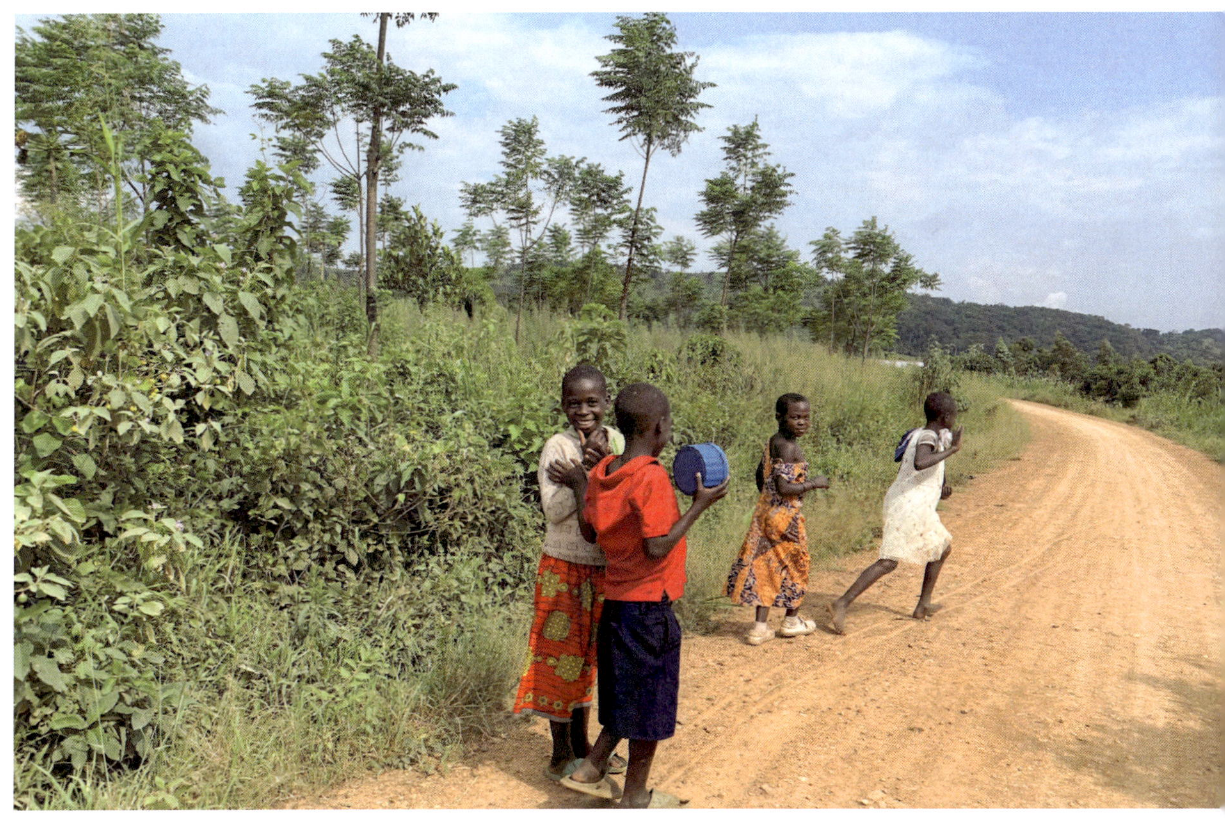

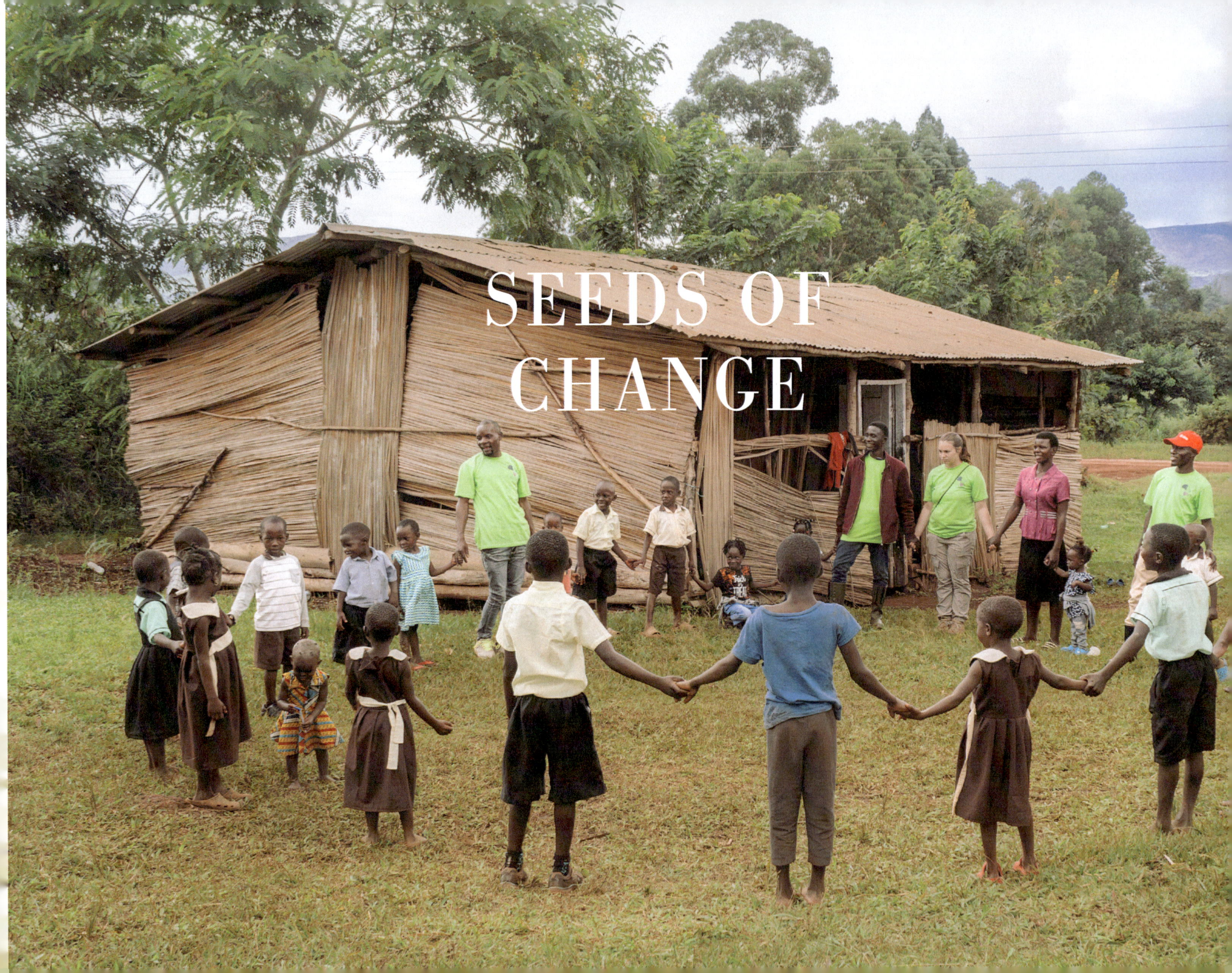

SEEDS OF
CHANGE

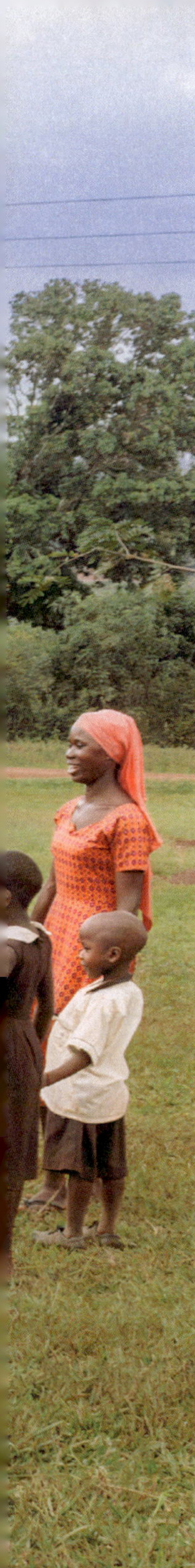

Planting Hope through Agri Planet Africa

Real change doesn't arrive with fanfare. It begins quietly—in the planting of a single seed, in the gathering of a community under the open sky, in the teaching of one person who will teach another. Across Uganda's fertile soils and refugee settlements, Agri Planet Africa plants more than crops; it plants hope, devotion, and a future that communities shape with their own hands. In every lesson shared and every seedling nurtured, there is a larger story unfolding—one of reclaiming dignity through knowledge, restoring the land through sustainable practices, and empowering leaders who will steward their communities toward lasting growth.

This chapter honors the quiet revolutions sparked by Agri Planet Africa: revolutions of soil, of spirit, and of shared purpose. It is a testament to what can grow when education is paired with opportunity, and when hope is planted not as charity, but as collaboration.

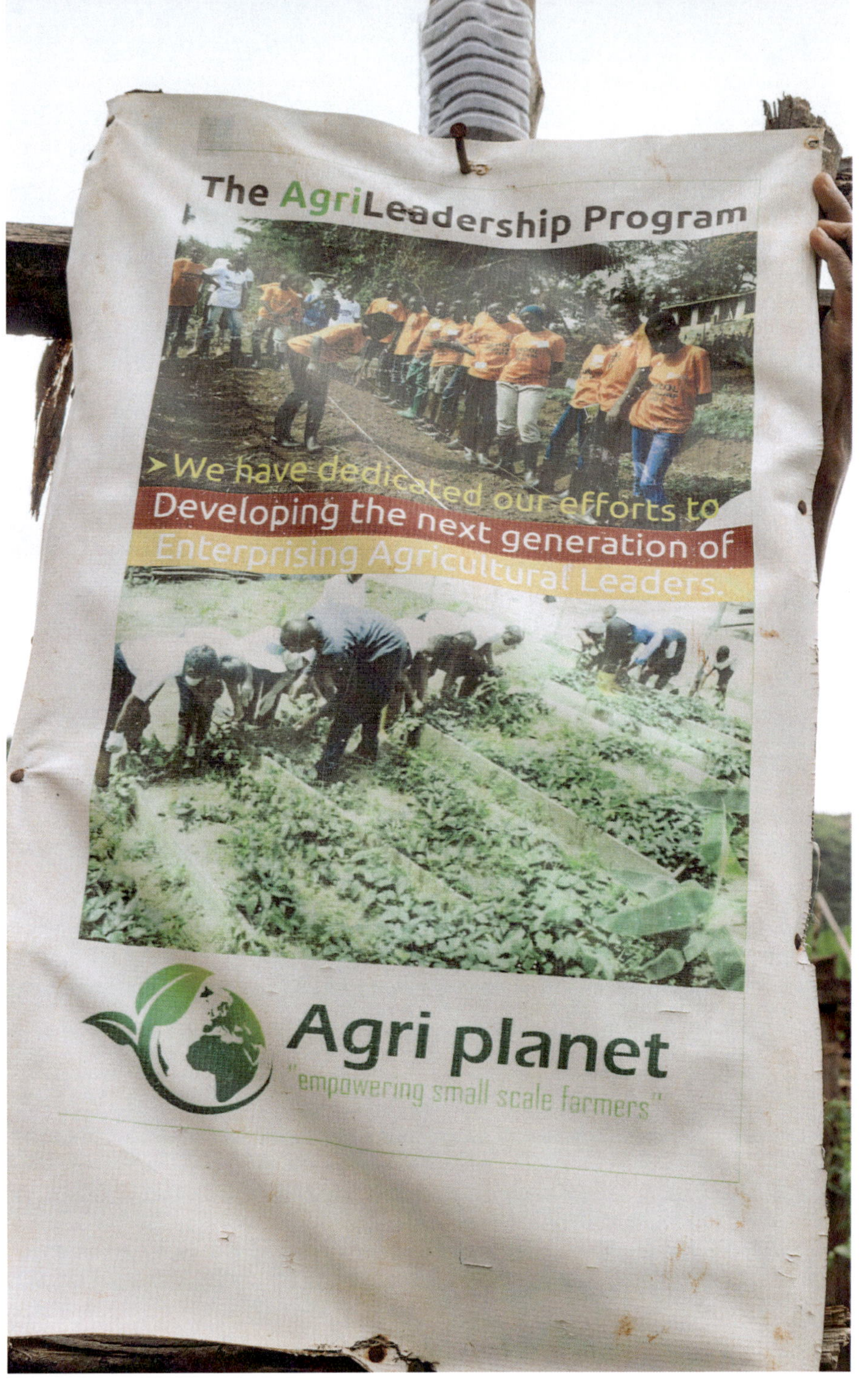

The Agri Planet Farms banner, proudly displayed at the Resource Center headquarters in Masindi, stands as a symbol of Agri Planet Africa's unwavering commitment to agricultural empowerment. Worn by time and the elements, it carries the message of the AgriLeadership Program, an initiative dedicated to developing the next generation of enterprising agricultural leaders.

This banner is more than just signage—it represents the promise of sustainable farming, education, and food security. Through hands-on training, innovative techniques, and a focus on community-driven solutions, Agri Planet Africa continues to empower small-scale farmers, helping them cultivate not just crops, but a future of hope, opportunity, and prosperity.

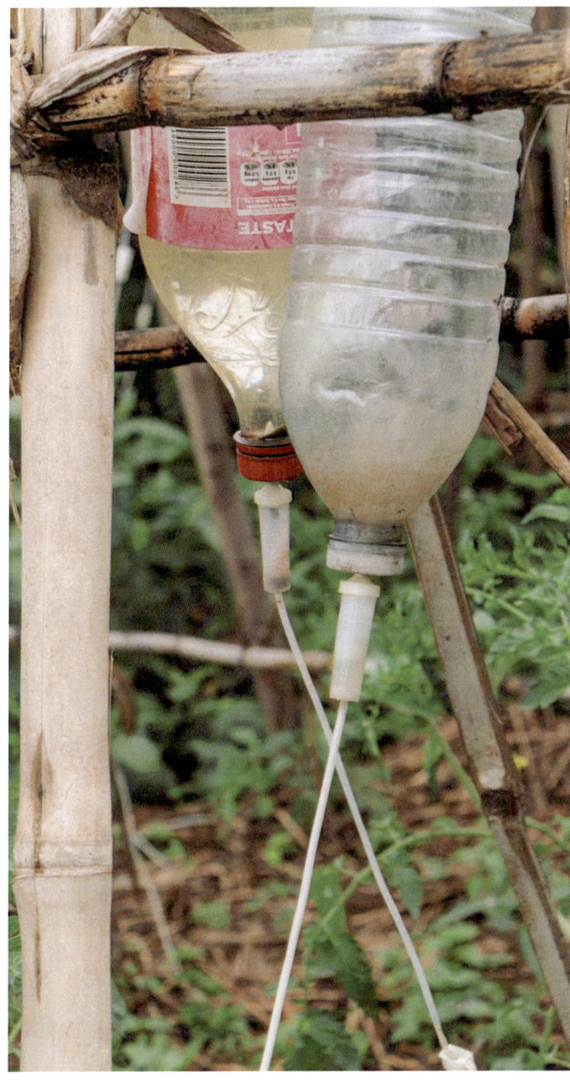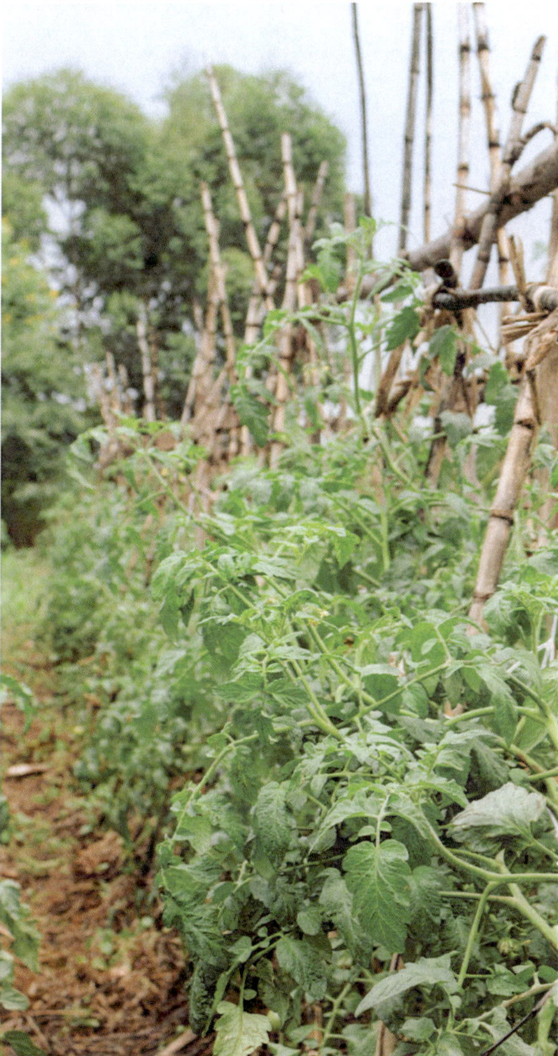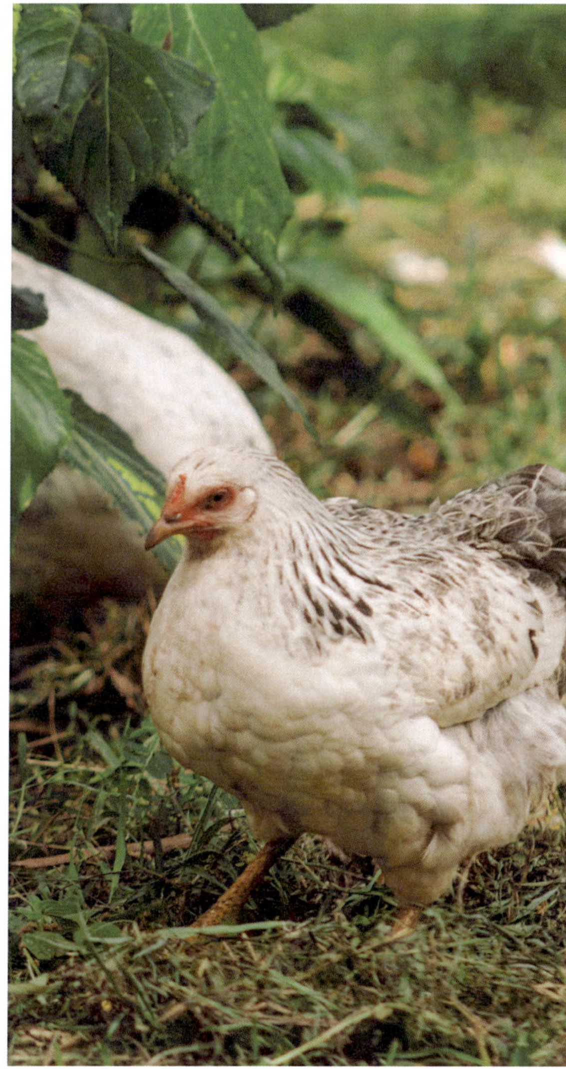

On the farms of Agri Planet Africa, sustainability is a rhythm—where nothing is wasted and everything has purpose. Plastic bottles become drip irrigation systems, feeding crops one patient drop at a time. Tomatoes rise in tidy rows, nourished by organic practices and the hands of those who farm with care. Even the chickens are part of the harmony—scratching the soil, clearing pests, and enriching the earth as they move. Together, these humble scenes reveal something extraordinary: that abundance grows wherever land, animals, and innovation work as one. Here, the future involves far more than planting as it is nurtured through intention, ingenuity, and deep respect for the land.

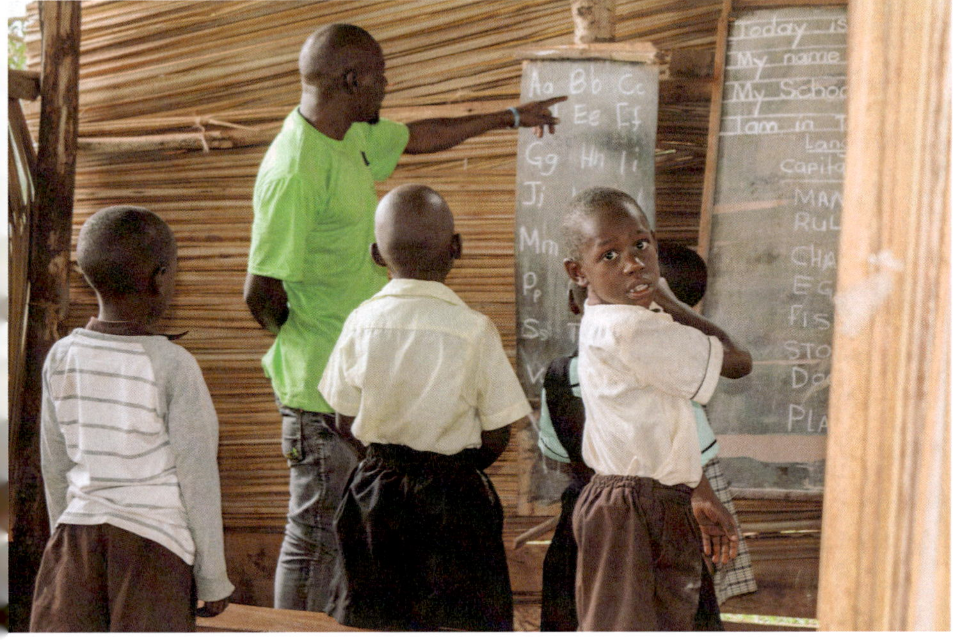

Before stepping into the fields, Agri Planet Africa began the day in the classroom—connecting with students and teachers at Saviour Junior Primary School and Orphanage to ensure that education remained central to their mission of sustainability.

In this moment, Ahaisibwe Brian (Atwooki), a volunteer with Agri Planet Africa, stands at the front of the class, guiding children through their alphabet. His presence is more than instruction—it is a symbol of how learning and agriculture grow best side by side.

Through foundational lessons like these, Agri Planet Africa empowers young minds with knowledge to shape their futures, just as they are equipped with tools to nourish their bodies through farming.

After the lesson, students joined the Agri Planet team to plant donated tree saplings, explore sustainable practices, and tour the farm. They learned how to cultivate tomatoes, apply organic manure, and harvest crops—skills that ensure the school can grow its own food for years to come.

This moment reflects Agri Planet's deeper purpose: to plant lasting seeds of knowledge, sustainability, and self-reliance that will continue to flourish for generations.

Kneeling in the rich Ugandan soil, Brian tends to a newly planted sapling outside Saviour Junior Primary School and Orphanage. His smile speaks of quiet pride—the kind that comes from knowing each small act can grow into something lasting.

This moment is more than planting a tree. It is planting possibility. Each sapling sown offers the promise of shade, nourishment, and cleaner air for generations to come. But beyond that, it plants hope—hope that with care and community, even the smallest seeds can reshape the future.

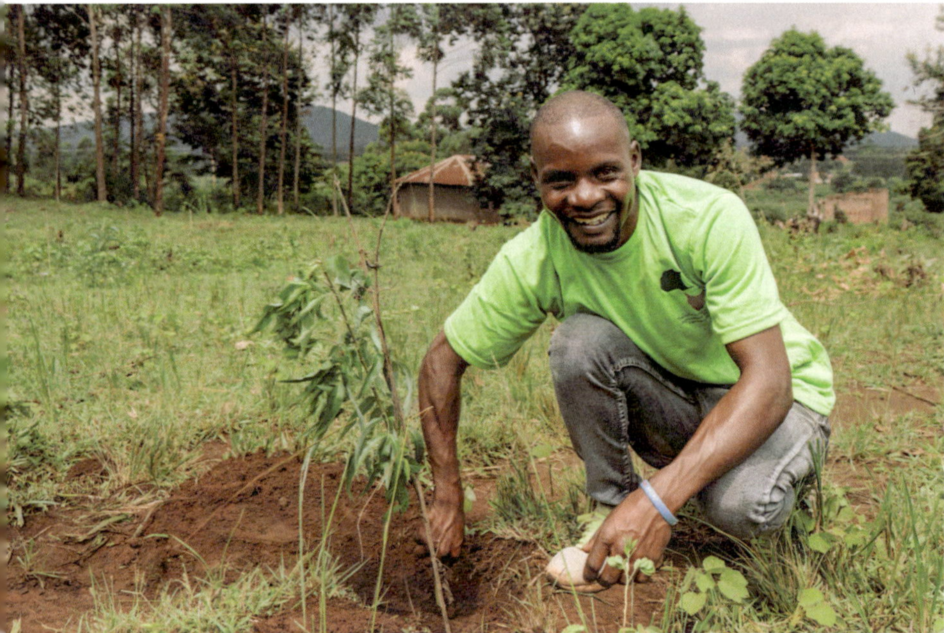

A young resident of Saviour Junior Primary School and Orphanage stands barefoot in the soil, her tiny feet pressing into the earth as her hands, guided by the gentle support of her teachers, grasp a young sapling. With quiet determination, she readies to place it into the soil just in front of her, an act both tender and powerful.

This moment, set against the backdrop of her home and school, is more than just planting a tree—it is planting a future. With each handful of soil, she and her community are nurturing growth, sustainability, and promise. One day, this tree will stand tall, offering shade, nourishment, and a reminder that growth, both for the land and for its people, begins with small, intentional acts of care.

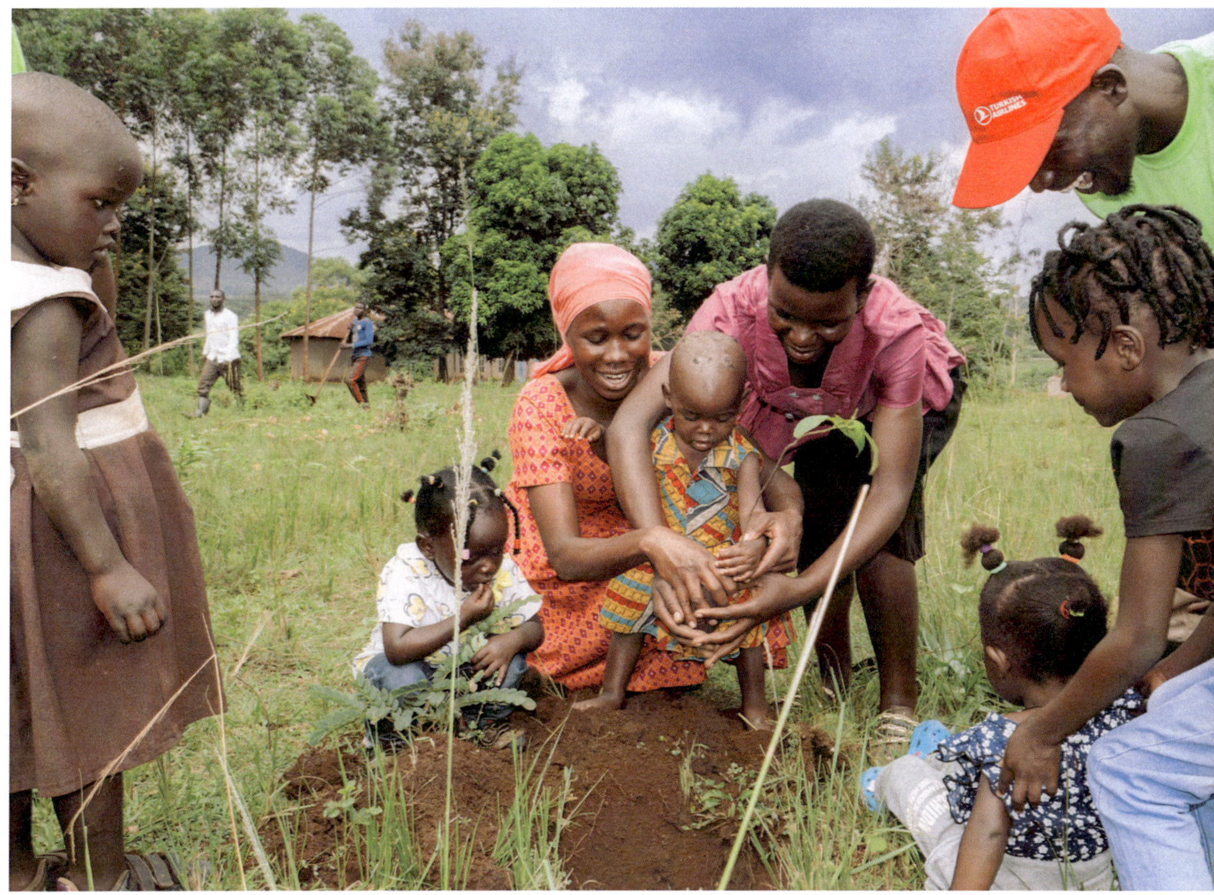

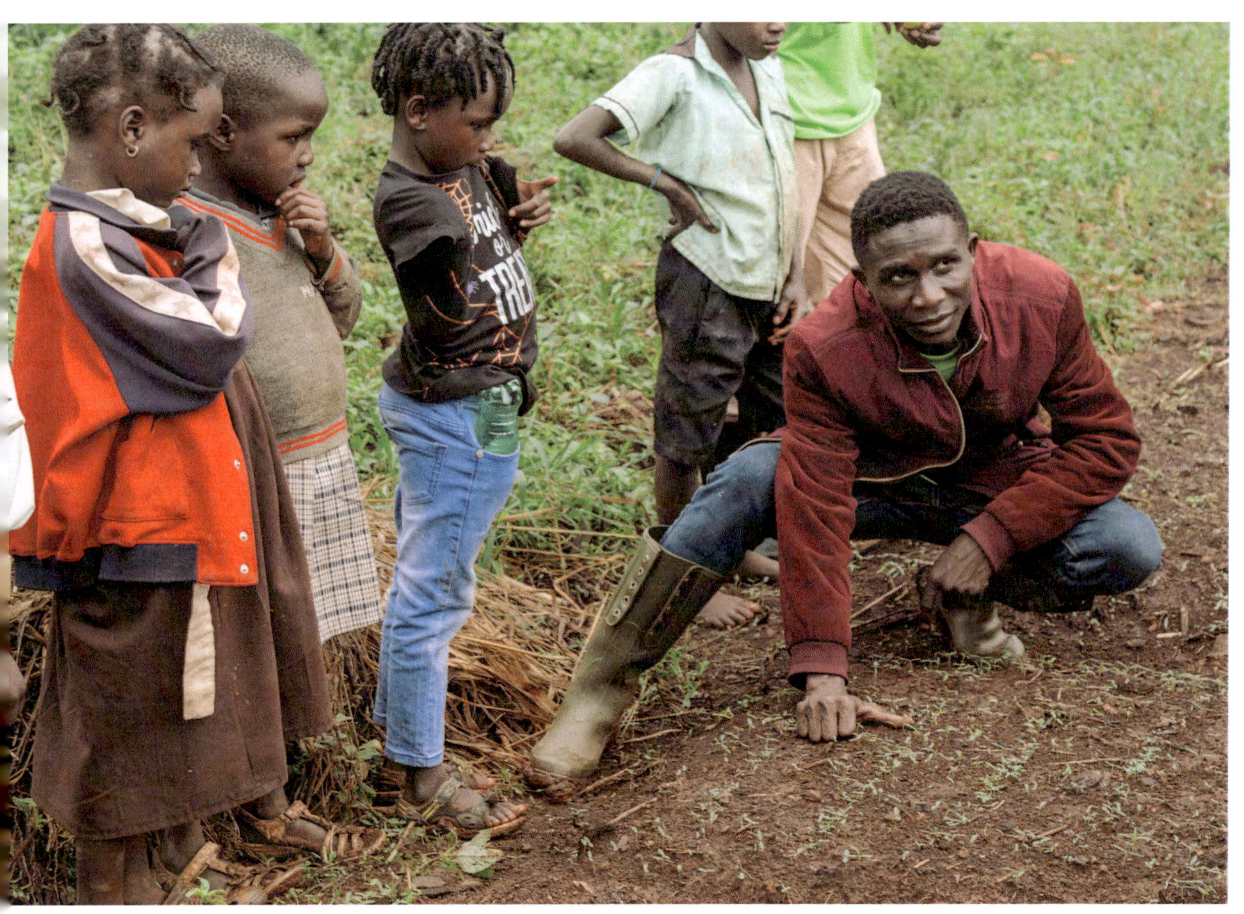

Cleofash demonstrates the precise technique of measuring the distance between seedlings, an essential step in ensuring healthy plant growth. While children eagerly observe, this lesson is primarily directed at their teachers, equipping them with the knowledge to reinforce sustainable agricultural practices in their classrooms and communities.

Taking place at the Agri Planet Africa farm, this moment embodies the core mission of Agri Planet: empowering local educators and farmers with the skills to cultivate small, productive farms that can sustain families for generations. By teaching best practices in spacing, soil health, and crop care, APA fosters long-term food security and agricultural stability.

Cleofash carefully pulls water from the rainwater collection system at the Agri Planet Africa Resource Center headquarters, demonstrating a sustainable approach to water conservation. The dome-shaped reservoir, designed to catch and store rainwater through the white PVC pipe leading from the roof, serves as a crucial lifeline for irrigation, drinking, and daily use. In a region where access to clean water can be challenging, this system represents resilience and ingenuity—transforming seasonal rains into a year-round resource. Around him, others observe, ready to learn and implement similar solutions in their own communities, reinforcing Agri Planet Africa's mission of self-sufficiency and sustainability.

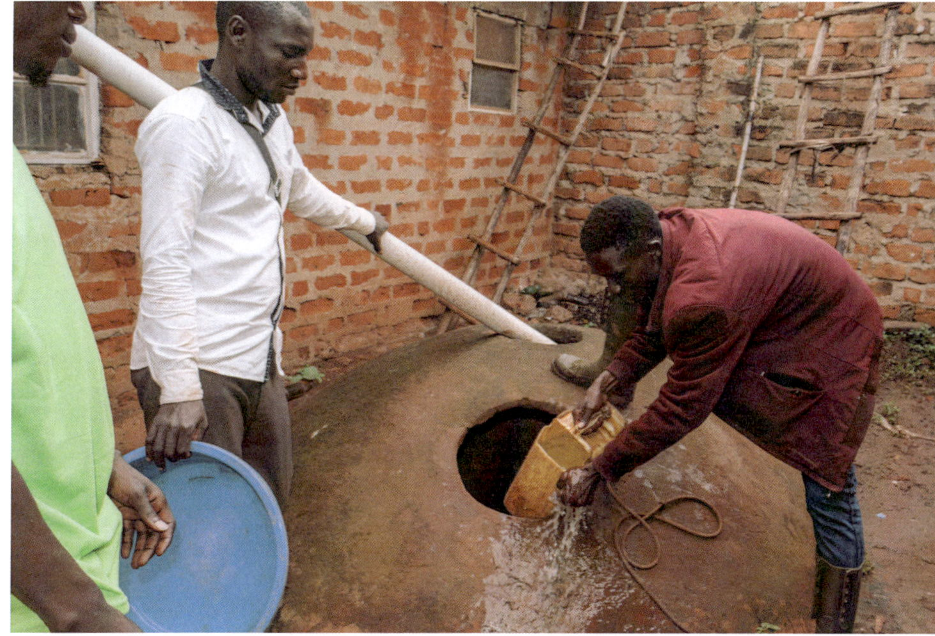

A pile of collected plastic bottles awaits transformation at the Agri Planet Africa Resource Center, where innovation and ingenuity meet necessity. Beside it, a rainwater collection system channels precious water through improvised piping—ensuring crops are nourished even in the driest seasons.

What others might see as waste, Agri Planet Africa sees as opportunity. These bottles will be repurposed into irrigation tools, helping farming communities safeguard their harvests and futures.

In this scene, Cleofash, one of Agri Planet Africa's dedicated leaders, stands as a quiet witness to the power of simple, sustainable solutions. Here, every action reflects a commitment to environmental stewardship, resourcefulness, and the belief that strength grows strongest when communities are empowered to use what they have.

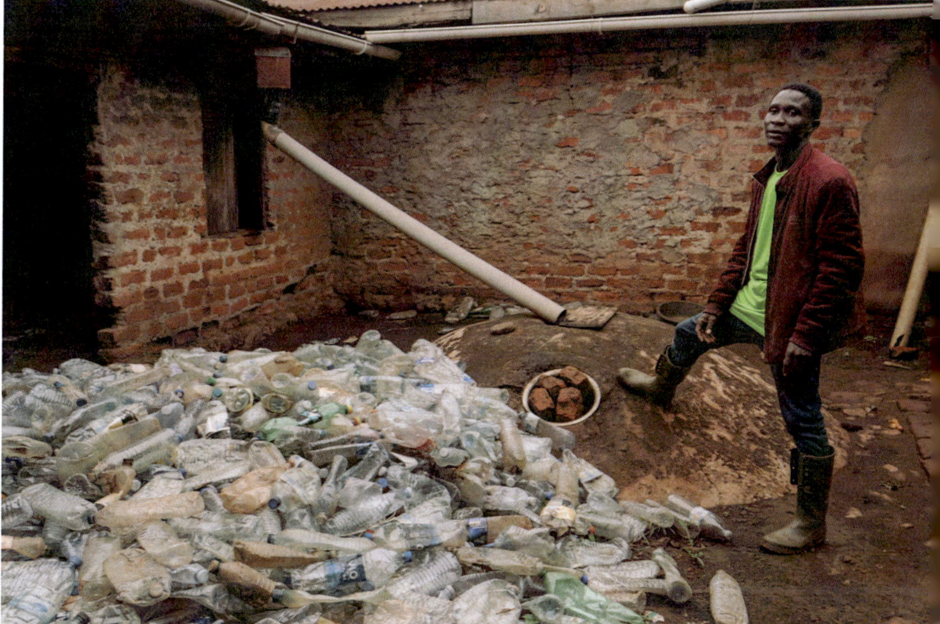

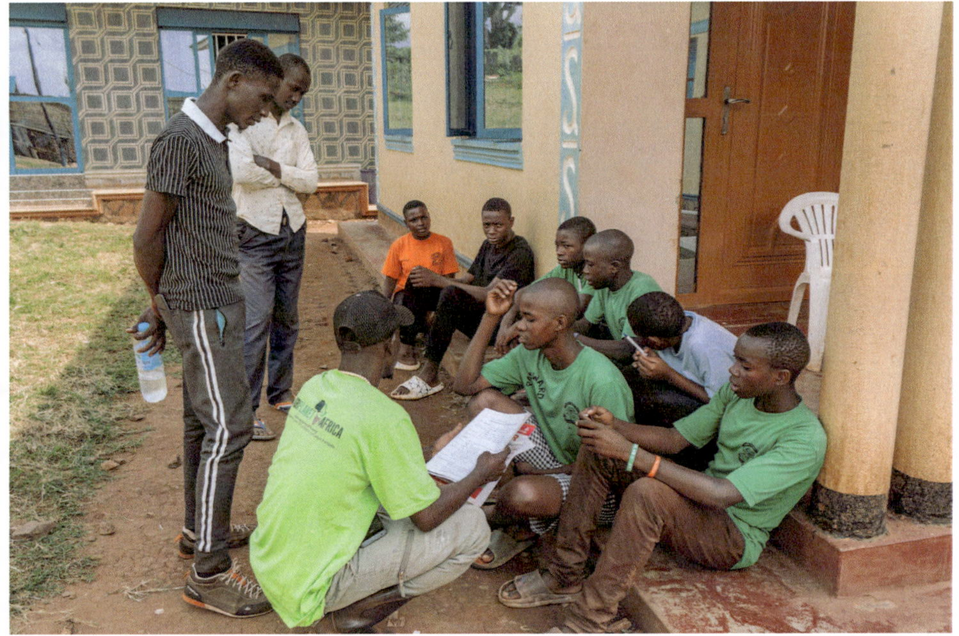

Seated on the steps of the volunteer dorms at Kyangwali Refugee Settlement, these students from COBURWAS International Youth Organization to Transform Africa (CIYOTA) are not just learning—they are building a vision.

With notebooks in hand and determination in their eyes, they present their agricultural business model to Agri Planet Africa's Ignatius and Cleofash, seeking practical feedback. More than just a class project, their plan is designed to create jobs, uplift their community, and foster self-reliance.

For these young minds, agriculture extends beyond planting crops to planting opportunities. With the right knowledge, resources, and mentorship, their ideas have the potential to transform their community, proving that innovation and progress thrive even in the most challenging environments.

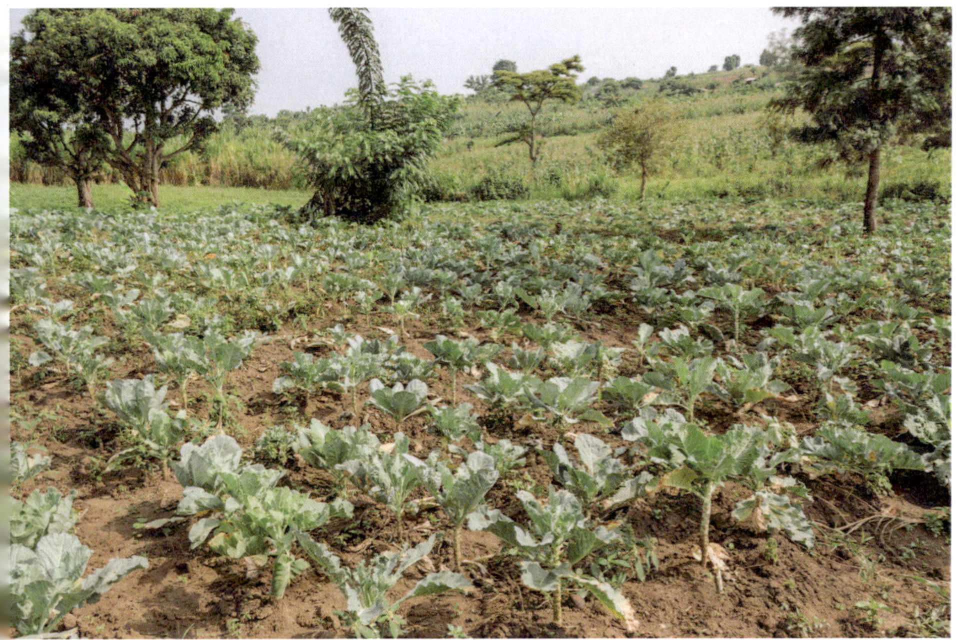

Nestled within Kyangwali Refugee Settlement, this thriving cabbage field stands as a powerful testament to sustainability and education. Years after Agri Planet Africa partnered with CIYOTA on a one-year agricultural training program, the results continue to nourish minds and bodies.

Originally established as a school garden, this project was designed to equip students with hands-on farming skills while also ensuring a reliable source of nutritious food. Today, the harvest provides meals for students, staff, and volunteers, reinforcing the idea that agriculture is more than just planting seeds—it is an investment in food security, self-sufficiency, and future generations.

What started as a simple initiative has grown into a living, learning farm, proof that when knowledge is planted, growth flourishes.

At the Agri Planet Africa Farms Resource Center, a quiet moment of connection embodies the heart of the organization's mission. During a hands-on agricultural training session, an orphan boy finds both safety and encouragement within the supportive arms of one of APA's founders, Ignatius. This image speaks to more than farming techniques; it captures a philosophy rooted in mentorship, empowerment, and nurturing the next generation. Training here is not just about planting seeds in the soil but about cultivating hope, confidence, and self-sufficiency, ensuring that every child has the opportunity to grow, learn, and flourish.

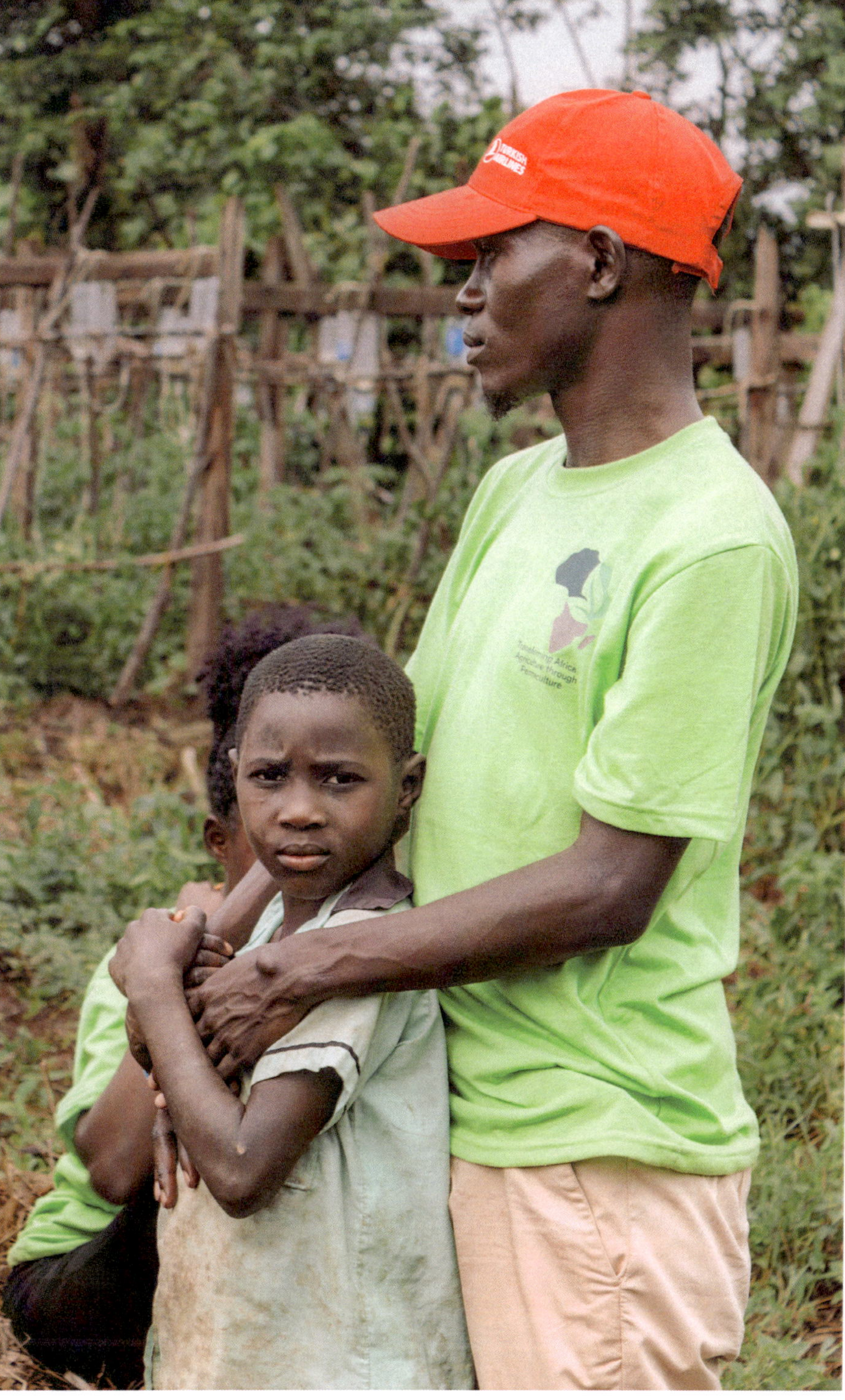

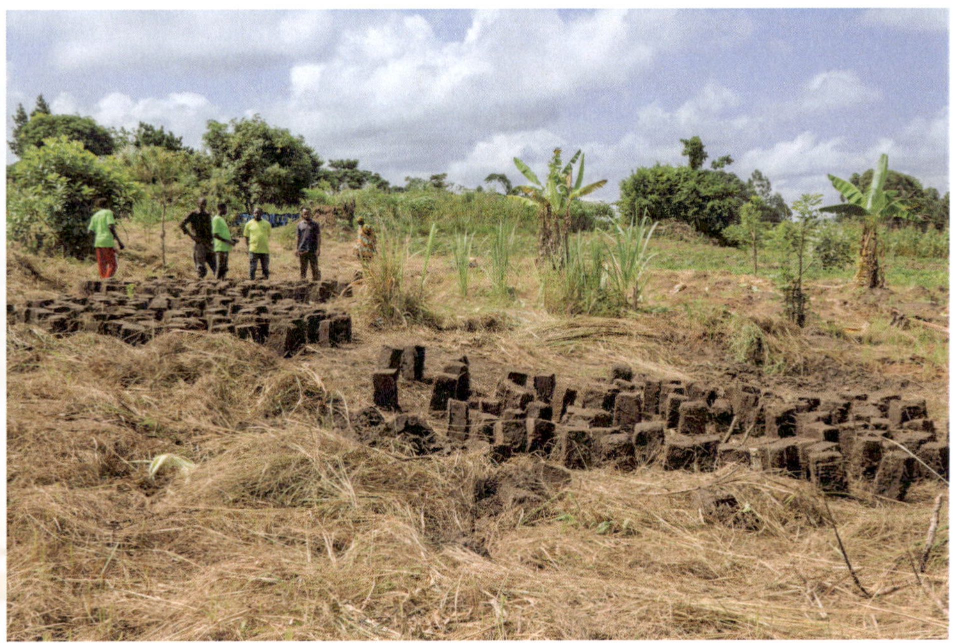

Scattered across the sunlit field, these handmade bricks are more than clay and earth—they are the foundation of a dream. Each brick, molded by hand and dried under the Ugandan sun, represents determination of a community coming together to build something lasting.

These bricks will soon form the walls of Agri Planet Africa's second Community Permaculture Resource Center in Kobusinge—a space where knowledge will be shared, farmers will be trained, and future generations will learn to sustain themselves.

Here, progress is tangible. It is built from the ground up, with the hands and hearts of those who believe in a better tomorrow.

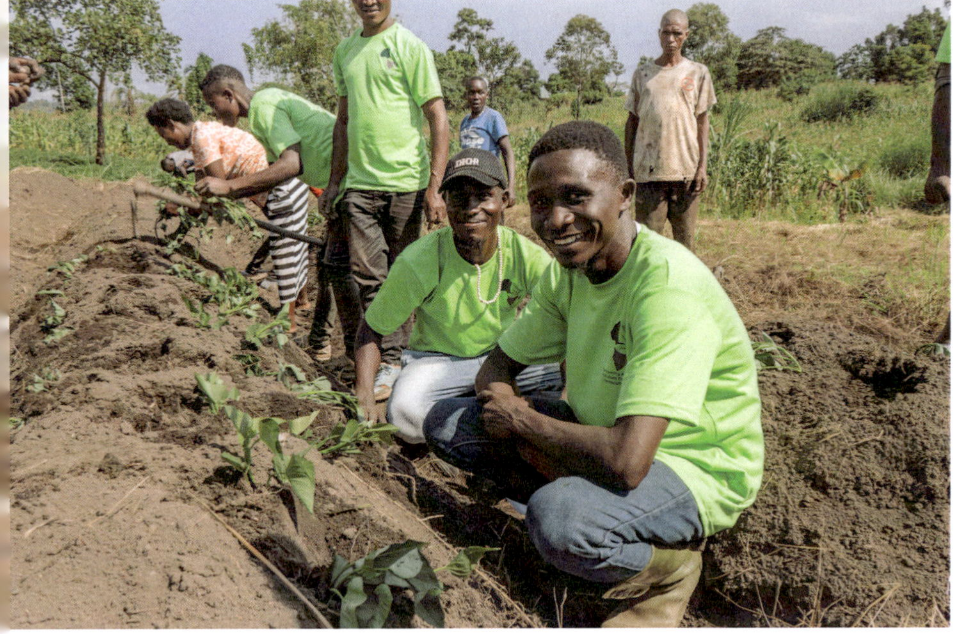

With warm smiles and soil-covered hands, Ignatius and Cleofash, the visionary co-founders of Agri Planet Africa, take a moment to pause from planting sweet potatoes—a symbol of both nourishment and sustainability. Behind them, the land is alive with movement. Volunteers and community members work side by side, digging, planting, and shaping the future of the Community Permaculture Resource Center. The sweet potato vines they place into the earth today will not only feed families but also serve as a living lesson in sustainable agriculture, teaching future generations the power of self-reliance.

This is more than just a farm. It is a movement—one rooted in hope, education, and transformation.

At the grand opening of Agri Planet Africa's second Community Permaculture Resource Center in Kobusinge, the community accomplished something extraordinary: 294 trees planted in a single day. Ahumuza Ignatius, CEO of Agri Planet Africa, stands at the heart of the gathering with quiet confidence, guiding volunteers and community members through the careful choreography of sustainable planning.

The selection tells its own story of thoughtful design: 153 Melia azedarach trees—known locally as Giant Lira—line the boundaries, creating natural fencing that will surge 1.7 meters (1.9 yards) annually among Uganda's fastest-growing boundary species. Forty-three pawpaw trees promise fruit and income within two years, while fifty-two eucalyptus trees stand ready as windbreaks and future timber. Six towering jackfruit trees will become landmarks, and forty banana trees will yield matoke, Uganda's beloved staple. Four rows of orange-fleshed sweet potatoes, rich in beta-carotene, stretch alongside nurseries of golden berries (high in vitamin C), tomatoes, bitter berries, and eggplants.

Ignatius, who has driven Agri Planet Africa's sustainable agriculture initiatives since 2015 and earned the prestigious Anzisha Grand Prize at just 21 years old, watches as his vision takes root. Here in the field, his influence is palpable. The crowd listens attentively, tools in hand, exchanging nods of agreement. This is more than planting—it is empowerment, a step toward food security and environmental restoration that will shape the land for generations to come.

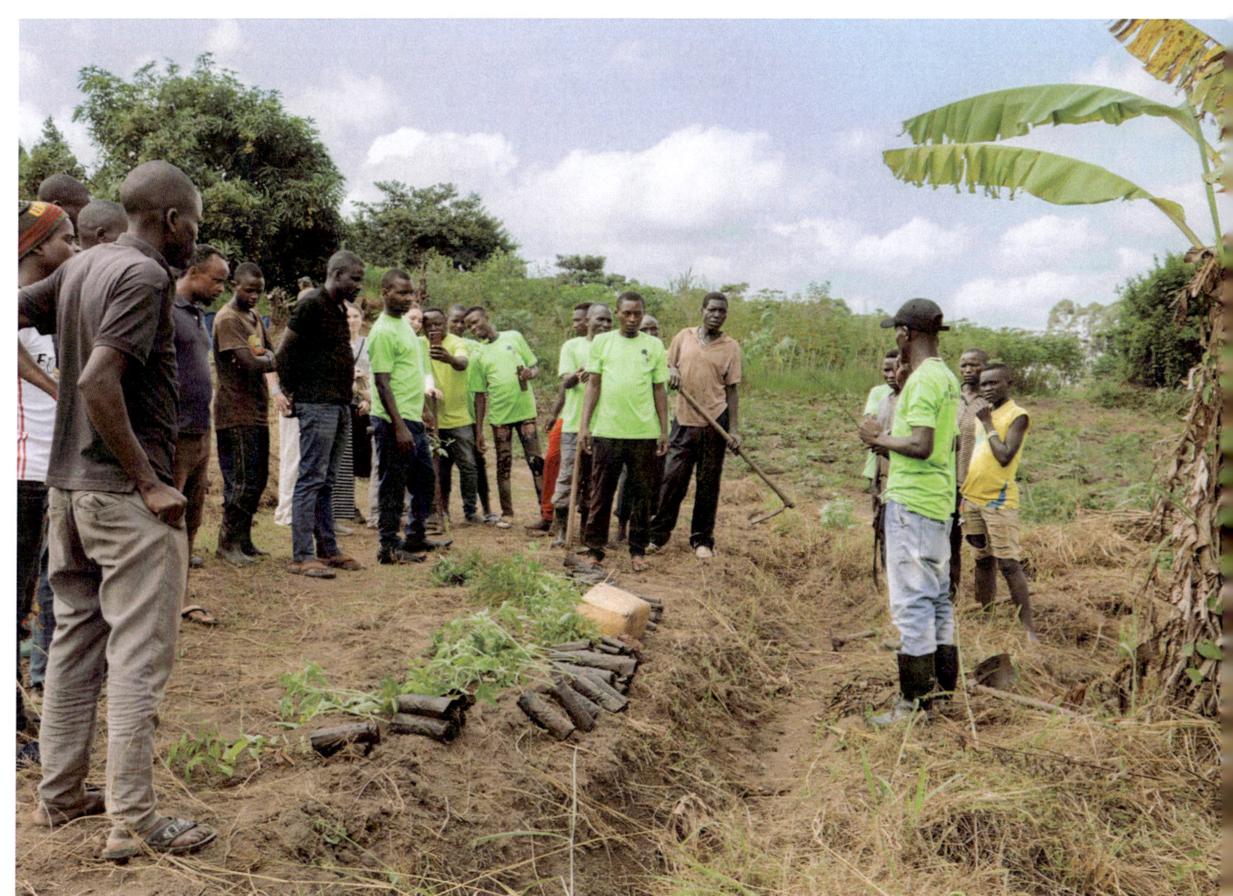

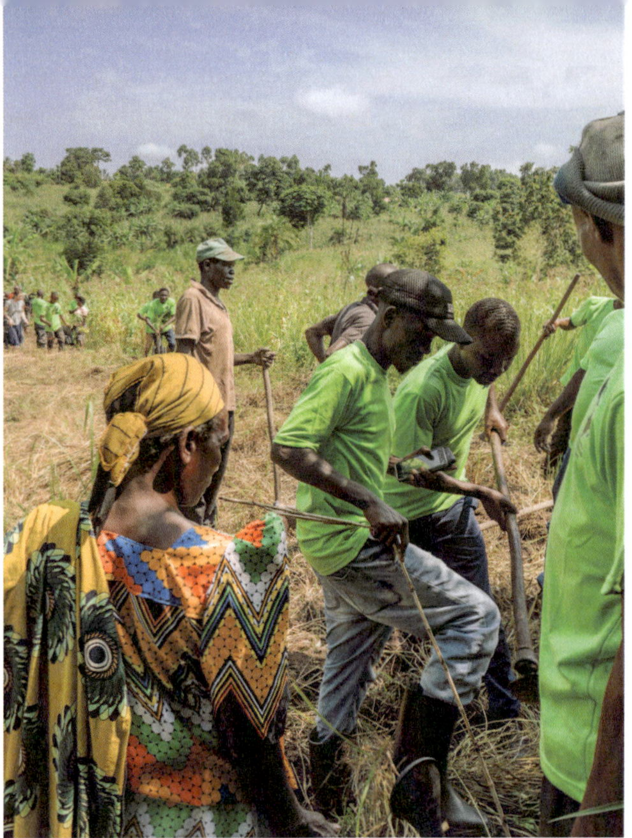

In the heart of Kobusinge, hands and tools meet the earth, turning over fresh soil in preparation for a new beginning. Ahumuza Ignatius, alongside dedicated volunteers, guides the community through the process of tilling the land—transforming this space into fertile ground that will soon bear fruit, both literally and metaphorically.

A woman in a vibrant gomesi watches the effort unfold, a silent witness to the change taking root. The rhythm of the hoes against the soil echoes a shared purpose, a belief that growth—whether in agriculture or in life— begins with collective effort.

This is more than farming. This is empowerment, transformation, and the foundation of a future where communities thrive through knowledge and sustainability.

With careful precision, Ignatius bends over a row of saplings, separating them with a touch that speaks of both knowledge and reverence. These fragile young trees, cradled in black plastic sleeves, hold the promise of shade, nourishment, and a thriving ecosystem. In this moment, he is more than a leader but is a cultivator of progress, a steward of sustainability.

Around him, the rhythm of the day continues—volunteers digging, planting, and nurturing the land. But this simple act, choosing and preparing each sapling for its new home, symbolizes something greater. It is the beginning of a story, where small hands plant big dreams, and where every tree in the soil is a declaration of hope for generations to come.

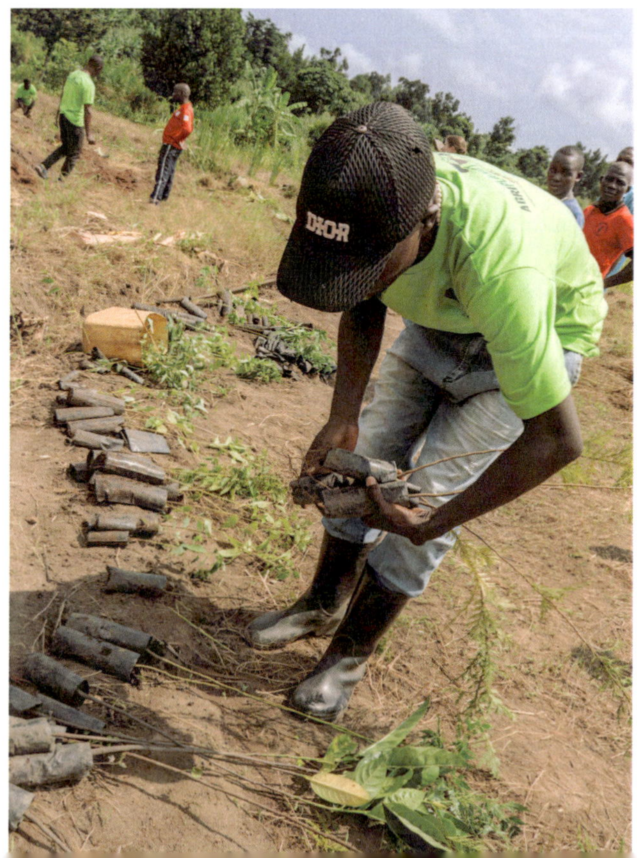

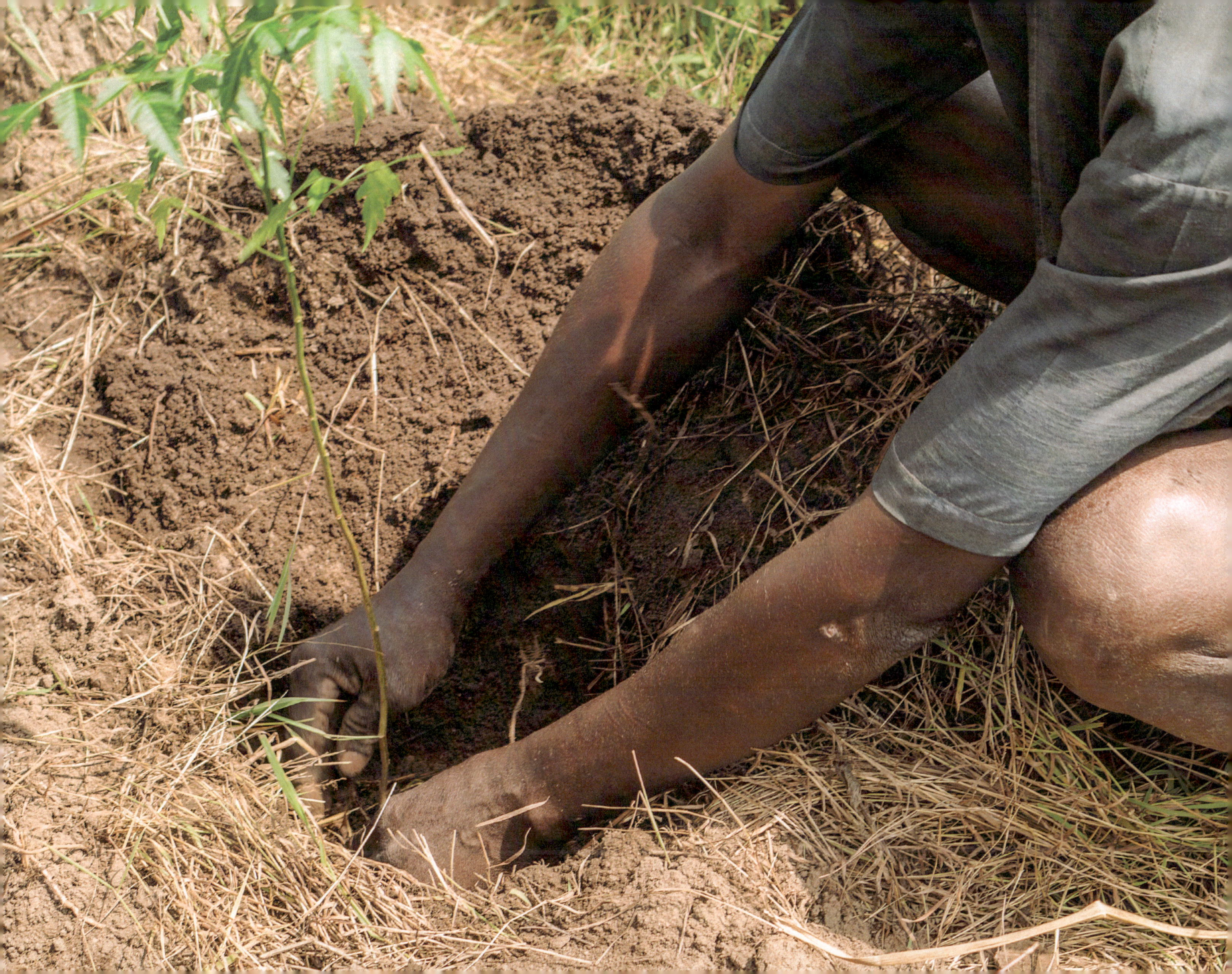

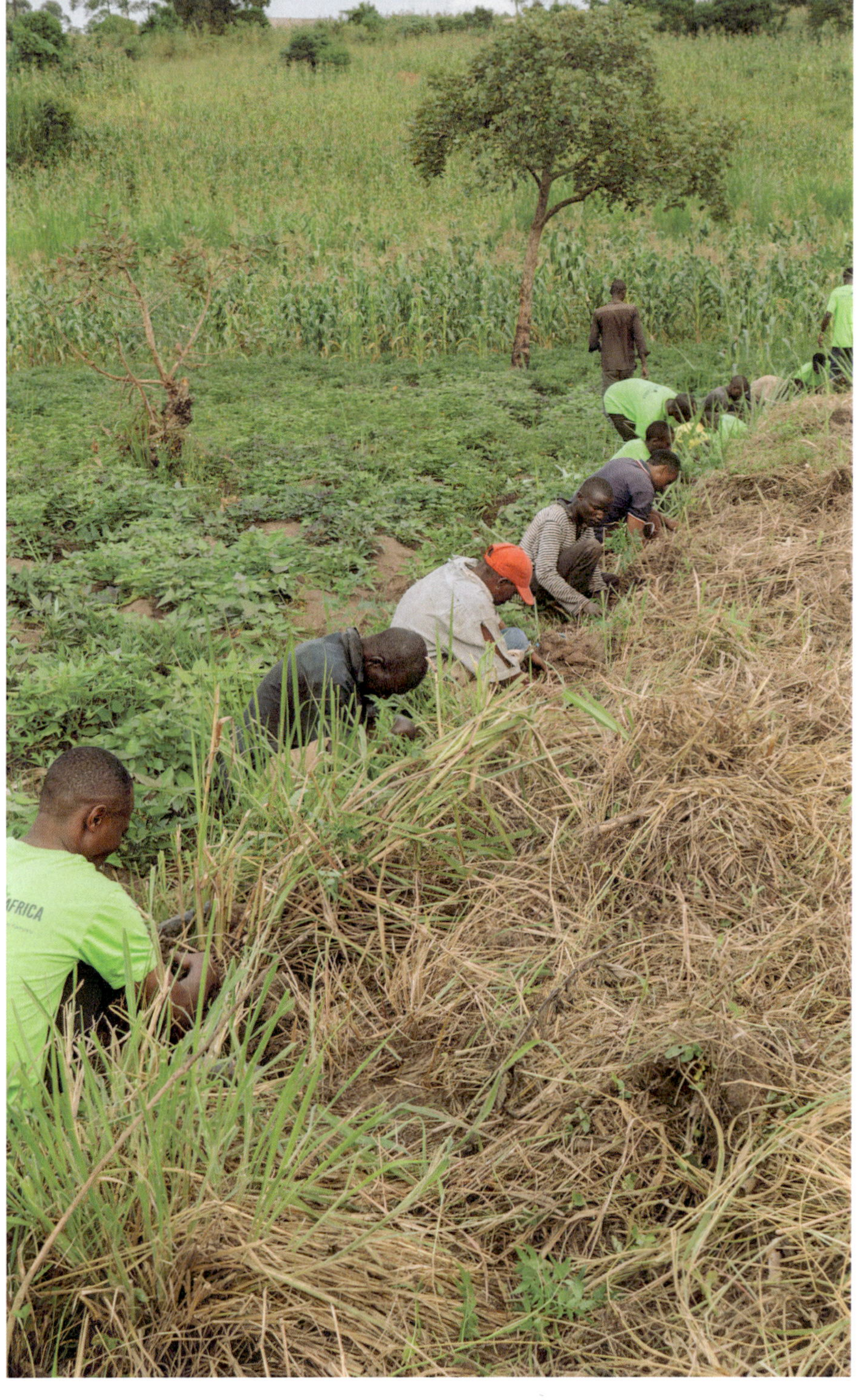

Hands deep in the earth, volunteers carefully place the first line of trees at the second Community Permaculture Resource Center in Kobusinge. This moment marks the beginning of something far greater than the trees themselves—it is the foundation of a thriving, sustainable future.

For the community and Agri Planet Africa, this was a defining step. Every seedling represents not just greenery, but food security, environmental conservation, and economic opportunity. The collective effort of volunteers working side by side shows the strength of community-driven change—where hope is planted as deeply as the roots of these trees.

Each seedling placed in the earth represented faith, shared purpose, and a commitment to growth.

With a bright smile and effortless grace, Shanita Allen Shanyz Komujuni carries logs to the site
where a fire will soon be kindled. The sun beats
down, but the weight of the wood is nothing com-
pared to the spirit she carries. In the background,
the lush Ugandan landscape stretches endlessly—a reminder of the richness this land offers
when nurtured with care.

After hours of planting in the pre-dawn coolness
before the day's heat arrived, Agri Planet Africa
ensures that volunteers are sustained not just by
purpose but by a warm, nourishing vegan meal
of beans, rice, and matoke—steamed bananas
that form Uganda's beloved staple dish. Shanita
plays a key role in preparing this communal feast,
a meal made with gratitude, community, and the
same hands that have just planted the seeds of
transformation.

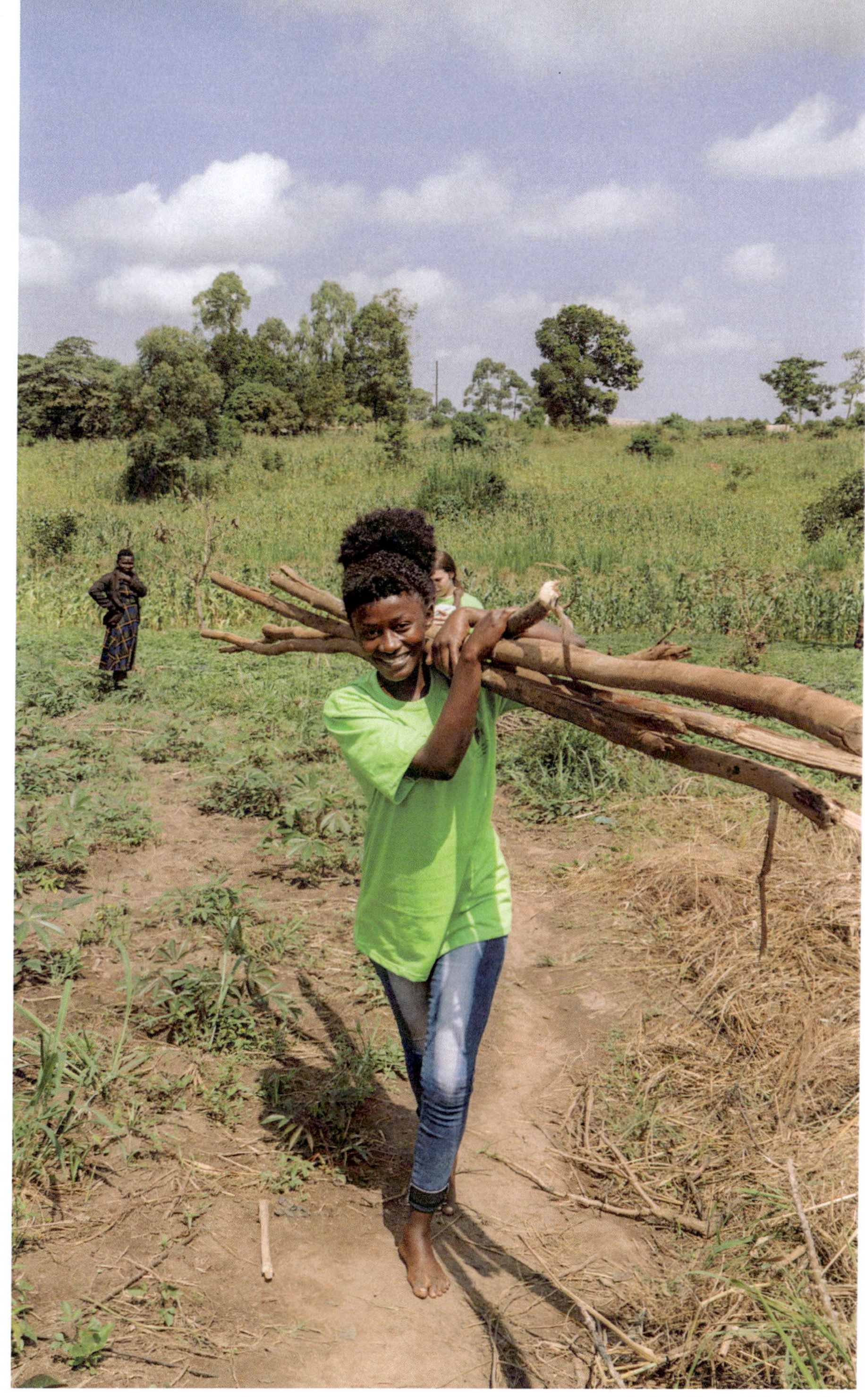

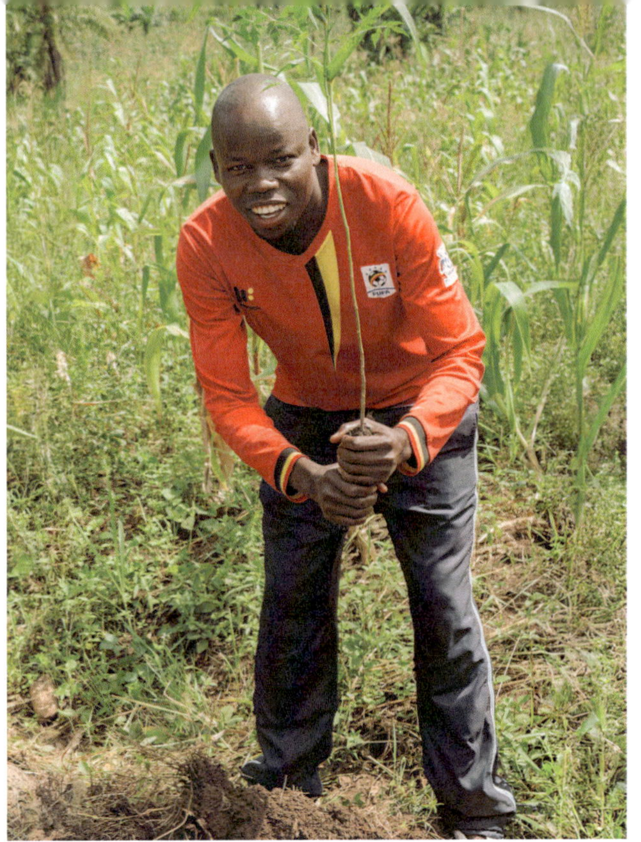

Dressed in the colors of Uganda, a volunteer from the local community holds a young sapling with both hands, ready to plant a tree that will stand for generations. His expression is one of pride, determination, and hope—capturing the spirit of community-driven reforestation.
Behind him, the land is alive with promise. With each tree planted, the community strengthens its relationship with the soil, knowing that this simple act carries the weight of food security, environmental protection, and economic sustainability.
Planting a tree becomes an investment in the future, one rooted in care and collective vision.

With a smile that mirrors the hope he's planting, a community volunteer carefully tends to rows of sweet potatoes at the newly established Community Permaculture Resource Center. His hands grip the tool with confidence, each movement embedding more than just crops into the soil—they plant resilience, self-sufficiency, and a future of abundance for the generations to come.
Sweet potatoes and yams, the large, starchy tubers quite different from what Americans call "yams," are staples in many Ugandan households, representing sustainability and nourishment. By cultivating them at the resource center, Agri Planet Africa ensures that nutritional security, agricultural education, and food sovereignty remain at the heart of the community's growth. Here, farming is more than labor, it is empowerment. Each mound of soil turned is a step toward independence, and each crop harvested will serve as both food and seed for future planting. This is how real transformation emerges.

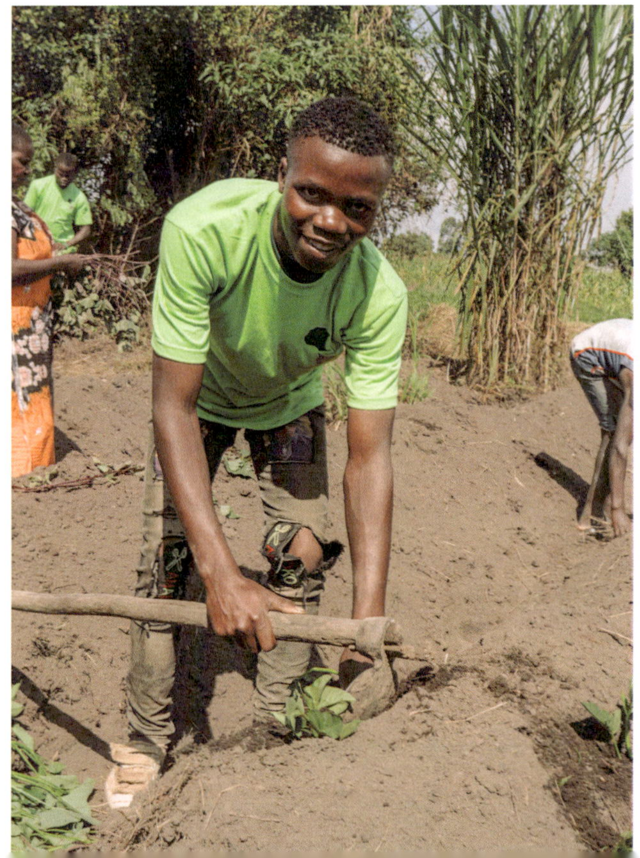

Beneath the shade of a mango tree, a circle of blue chairs forms a space for voices to rise, ideas to flow, and solutions to take root. As Ignatius and the Agri Planet Africa team engage in conversation with community members, some pluck ripe mangoes from the branches above—a simple yet symbolic act of harvesting knowledge alongside fruit. This is more than a meeting; it is a dialogue of empowerment. The community asks insightful questions, sharing concerns and aspirations. One pressing issue is seed fraud—where farmers are sold defective seeds that never sprout, leading to devastating losses. In response, Agri Planet Africa introduces its seed bank initiative, a system built on trust and sustainability. The program ensures that farmers receive high-quality seeds, grown and harvested by APA itself. In return, those who borrow seeds repay only with an equal amount— or, if able, a little extra—to keep the cycle thriving. This gathering is a testament to collaboration— where knowledge is exchanged as freely as the shade under this tree, and where hope is planted alongside crops that will sustain generations.

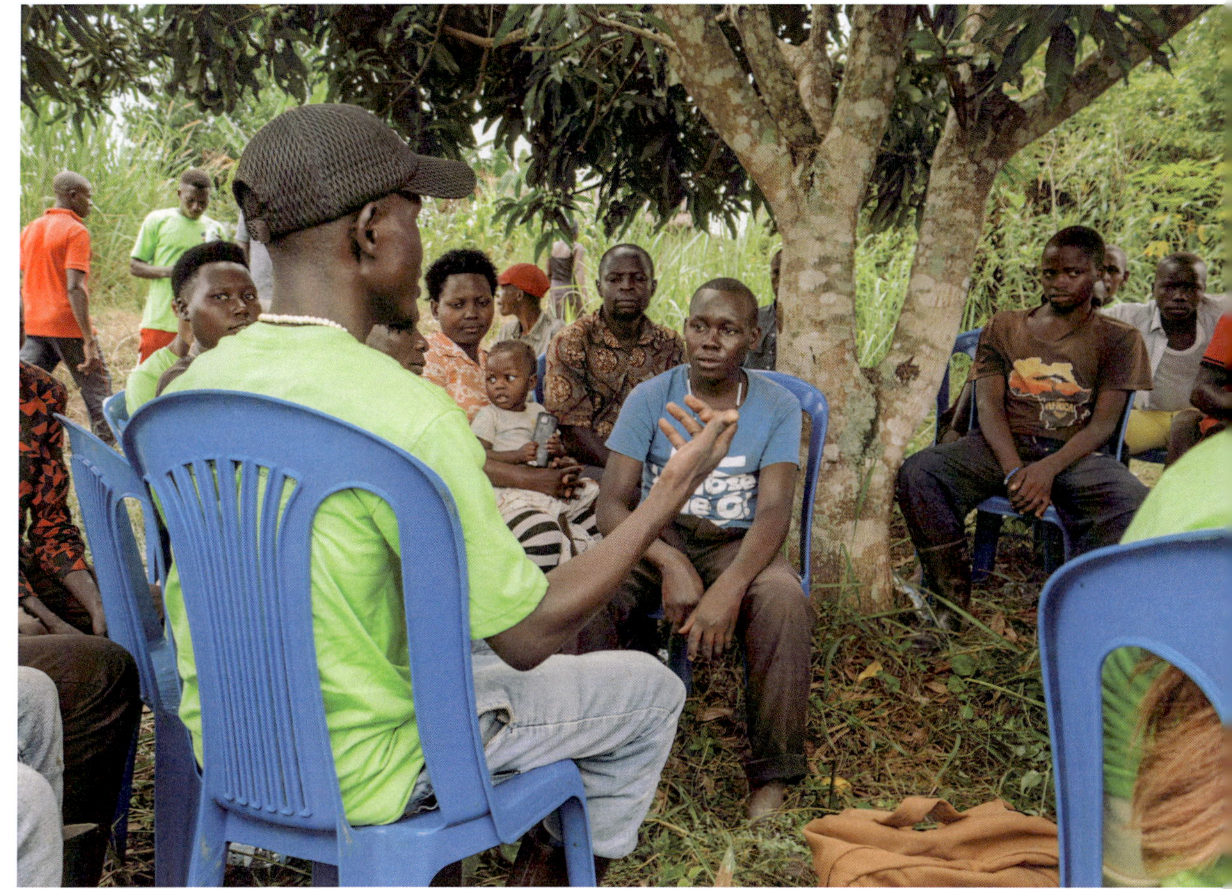

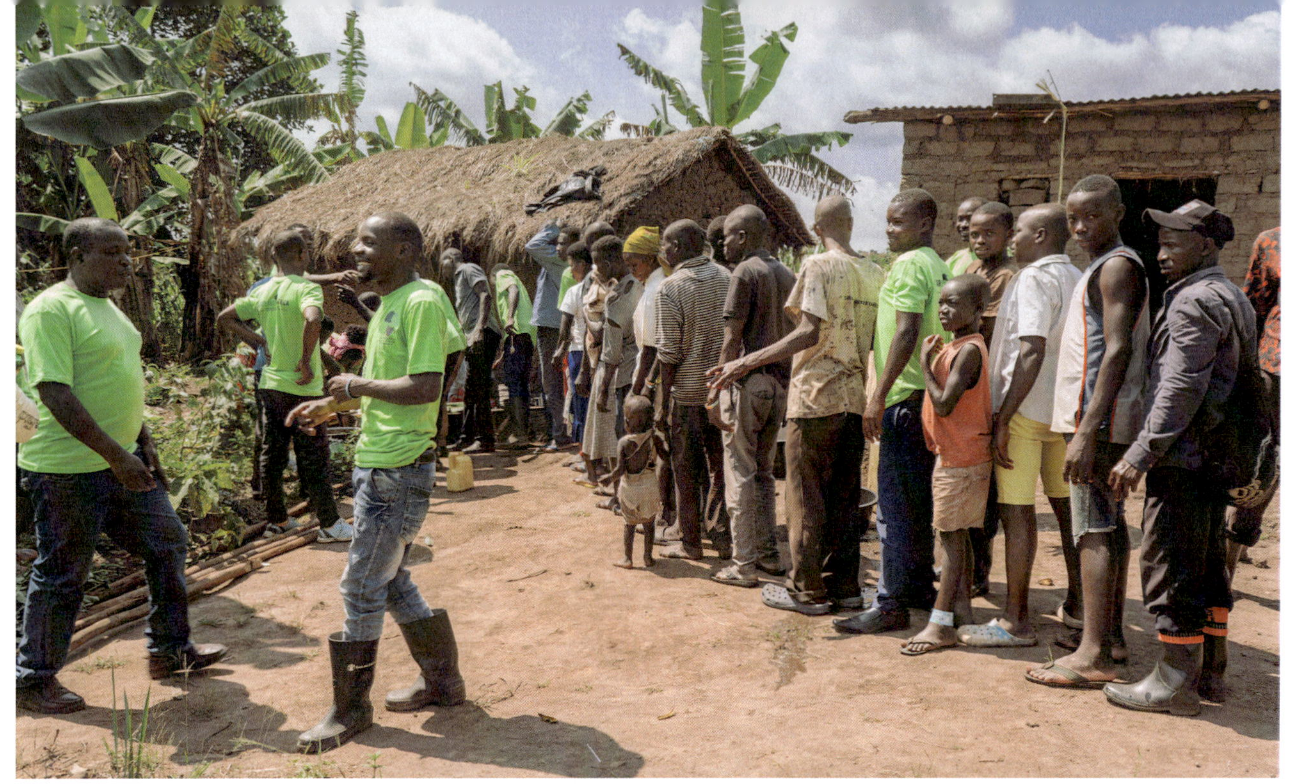

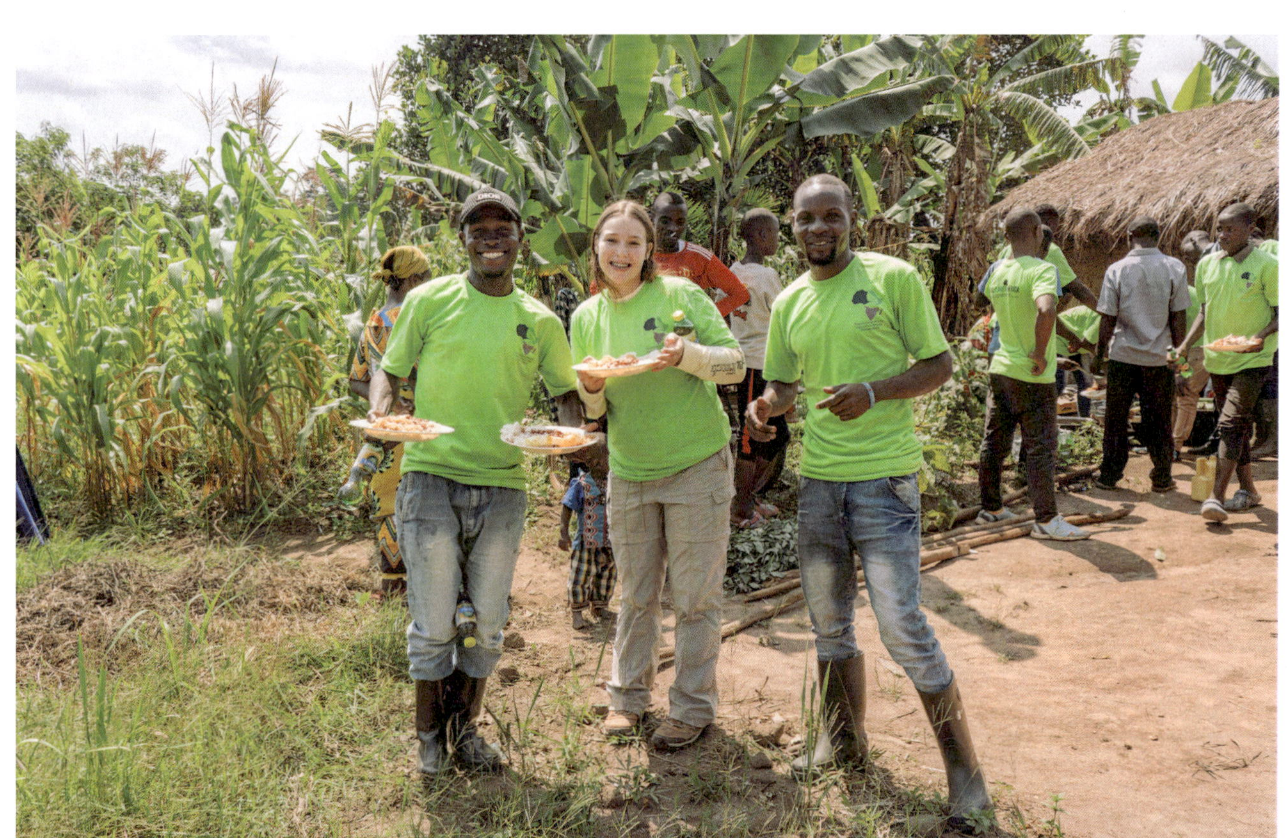

As the sun casts warm golden light over the newly established Community Permaculture Resource Center, the day's hard work ends with shared gratitude; a communal meal hosted by Agri Planet Africa and prepared by local hands. Lined up patiently, volunteers and community members gather to receive their portions of beans, rice, and matoke, a staple dish made from steamed bananas, the rich aromas mingling with the earthy scent of freshly turned soil.

While this community had encountered white people before, though infrequently, the familiar dynamics still played out: younger children reaching tentatively to hold our hands, teenagers and young adults eagerly seeking photos together, while elders maintained a more reserved, sometimes skeptical distance. In several other rural communities we visited during our trip, particularly where few laughed and we were the first *mazungu* (white people) some had ever seen, the curiosity could become overwhelming. I remember when we blew a tire in one remote location, we had to find a quiet place to wait while it was repaired, as crowds began gathering with an intensity that could have stirred unintended agitation in the community. Yet here in this village, the warmth was immediate and manageable… a testament to the relationships Ignatius had cultivated long before our arrival.

The decision to serve a vegan meal was a nod to my Buddhist principles, honoring both nourishment and sustainability while reflecting Agri Planet Africa's mission to cultivate food and lasting connections across all cultural boundaries.

Laughter and gratitude fill the air as the simple meal of rice, beans, and matoke represents far more than nourishment; it embodies the unity and shared effort that made this day possible.

This scene reflects the intentional leadership structure of Agri Planet Africa: an organization founded and directed by Ugandan nationals who understand their communities' needs intimately. When they appointed me as Executive Director, it was based on complementary skills, not external intervention. Trust here isn't built through grand gestures, but through daily proof that outsiders can follow rather than lead. For Lena, having traveled from the United States, this moment represents something profound about authentic partnership. She sits not as a benefactor, but as a student among teachers who happen to be farmers, community organizers, and visionaries.

Reflecting on the experience now at 18, two years after that transformative trip at 16, Lena shares: *"I was nervous at first, but everyone made us feel like family from day one. The little kids would grab my hand and show me everything, and the adults taught me farming techniques.*

I remember pigs and goats tied up by the roadside, valued for trading and breeding, and the incredible jackfruit picked fresh from the trees. Everything became part of the daily life they welcomed me into.

Meeting baby Janelle, named after my mom, showed how deep these connections go. I came thinking I might help, but they taught me far more about community and what really matters."

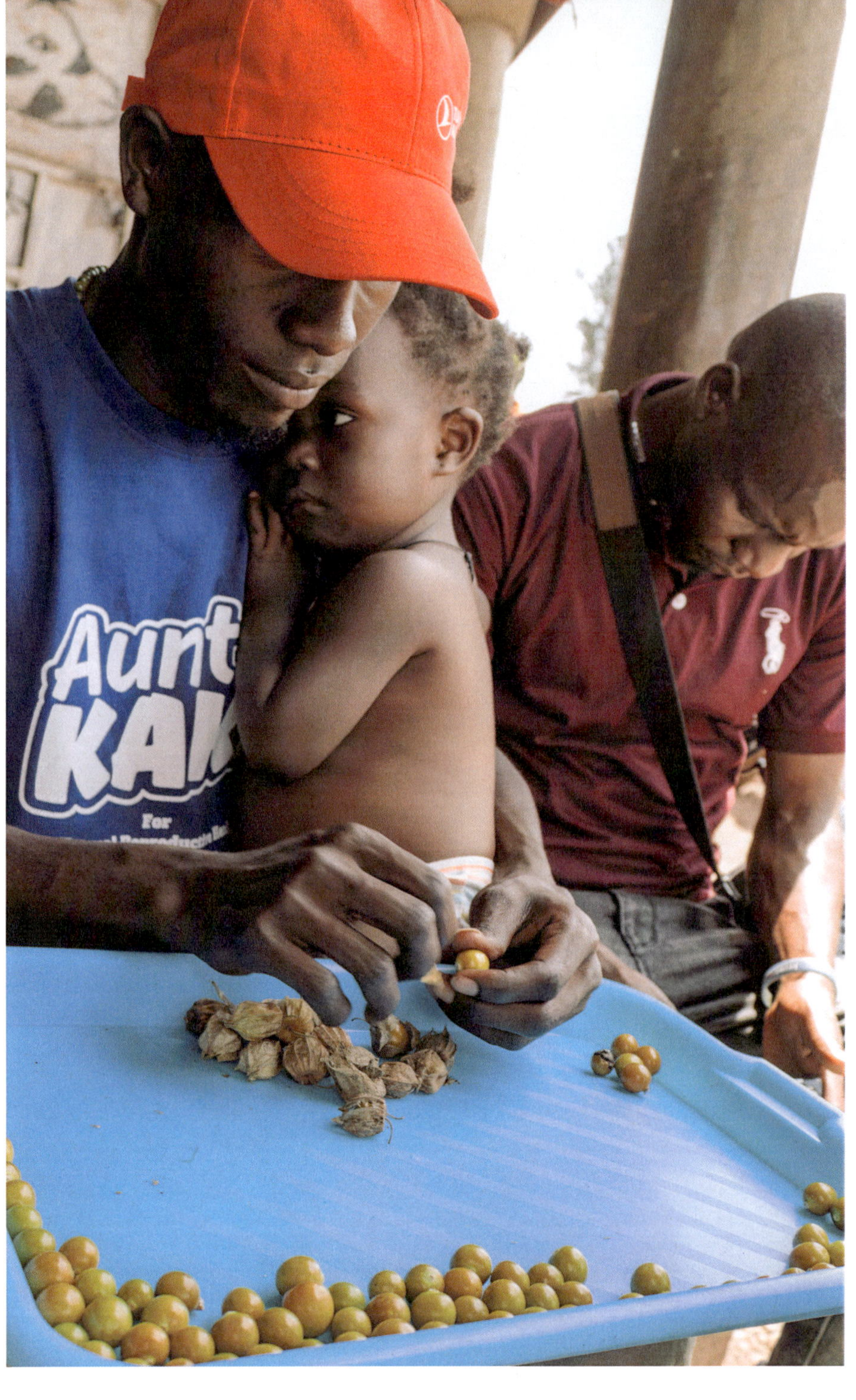

Ignatius holds his daughter, Janelle, while husking freshly harvested golden berries from Agri Planet's golden berry farm. He sits with her at the Agri Planet Grocers, carefully peeling back the husks while Cleofash cuts labels, both working methodically to clean and package the berries for immediate delivery to existing and potential new customers. The golden berry farm is situated a ten-mile walk from the grocers, a journey that winds through dense bush, past towering pine trees, and between villages and towns. The berries are carried by hand, making their way first to the grocers and then onward to awaiting buyers. Some berries are pre-ordered for delivery, while others are sold along the way, turning the long trek into an opportunity for commerce and connection. As the primary caretaker of the headquarters resource center and grocers, Cleofash ensures the smooth operation of this process, managing the harvest and distribution. Golden berries, rich in nutrients, are more than just produce—they are a vital source of nourishment for those with limited access to continuous nutrients, reinforcing Agri Planet Africa's mission to provide sustenance and sustainability to the communities it serves.

Standing in front of Agri Planet Grocers, Cleofash, Brian, Lena, and Ignatius represent more than just a team—they embody a vision of fair trade, sustainability, and community-driven agriculture. This market serves as a critical link between Agri Planet Africa's farms and local consumers, ensuring that fresh, organic produce reaches the people who need it most. But its impact goes deeper. Agri Planet Grocers provides a fair and reliable marketplace for farmers within APA programs, protecting them from exploitation and ensuring they receive just compensation for their hard work.

From the hands that plant the seeds to the hands that carry the harvest home, this initiative ensures that agriculture remains a source of dignity, opportunity, and nourishment for the community.

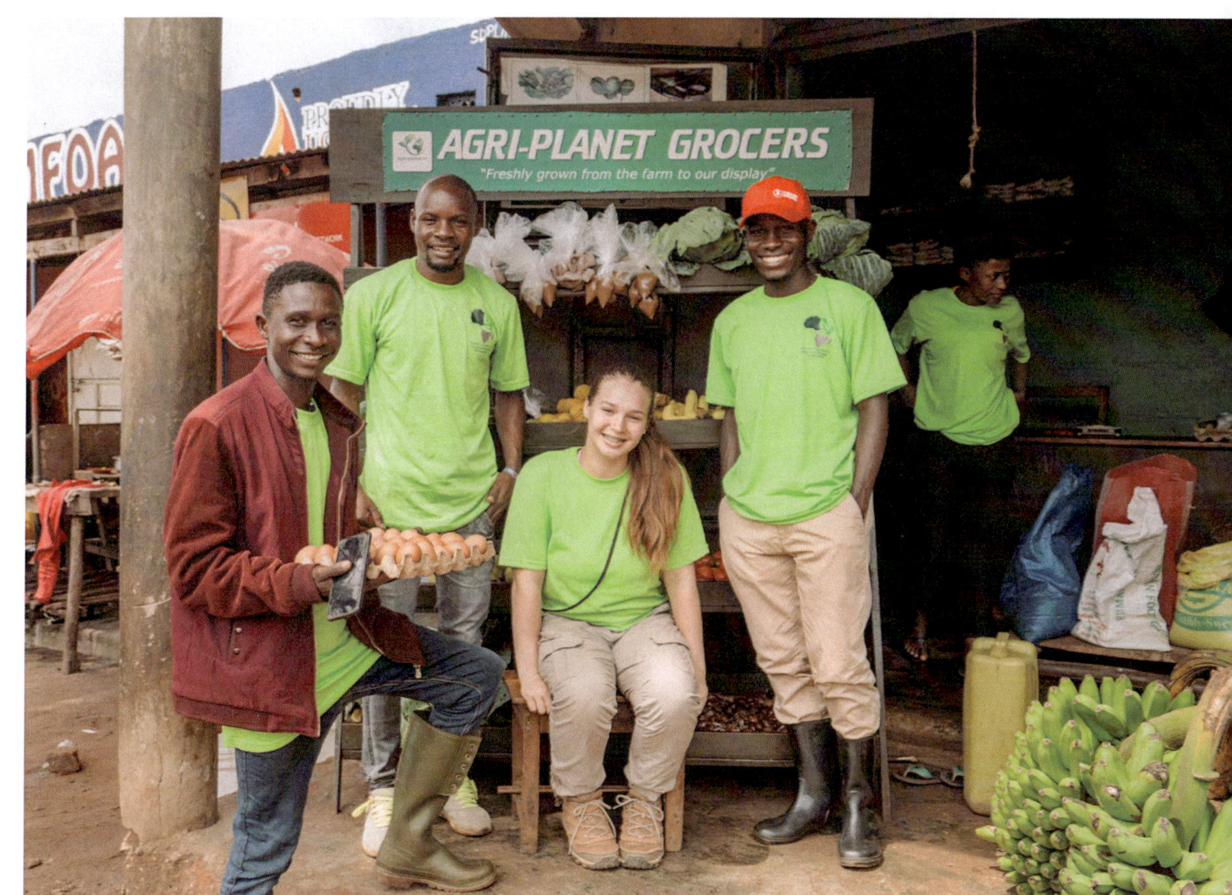

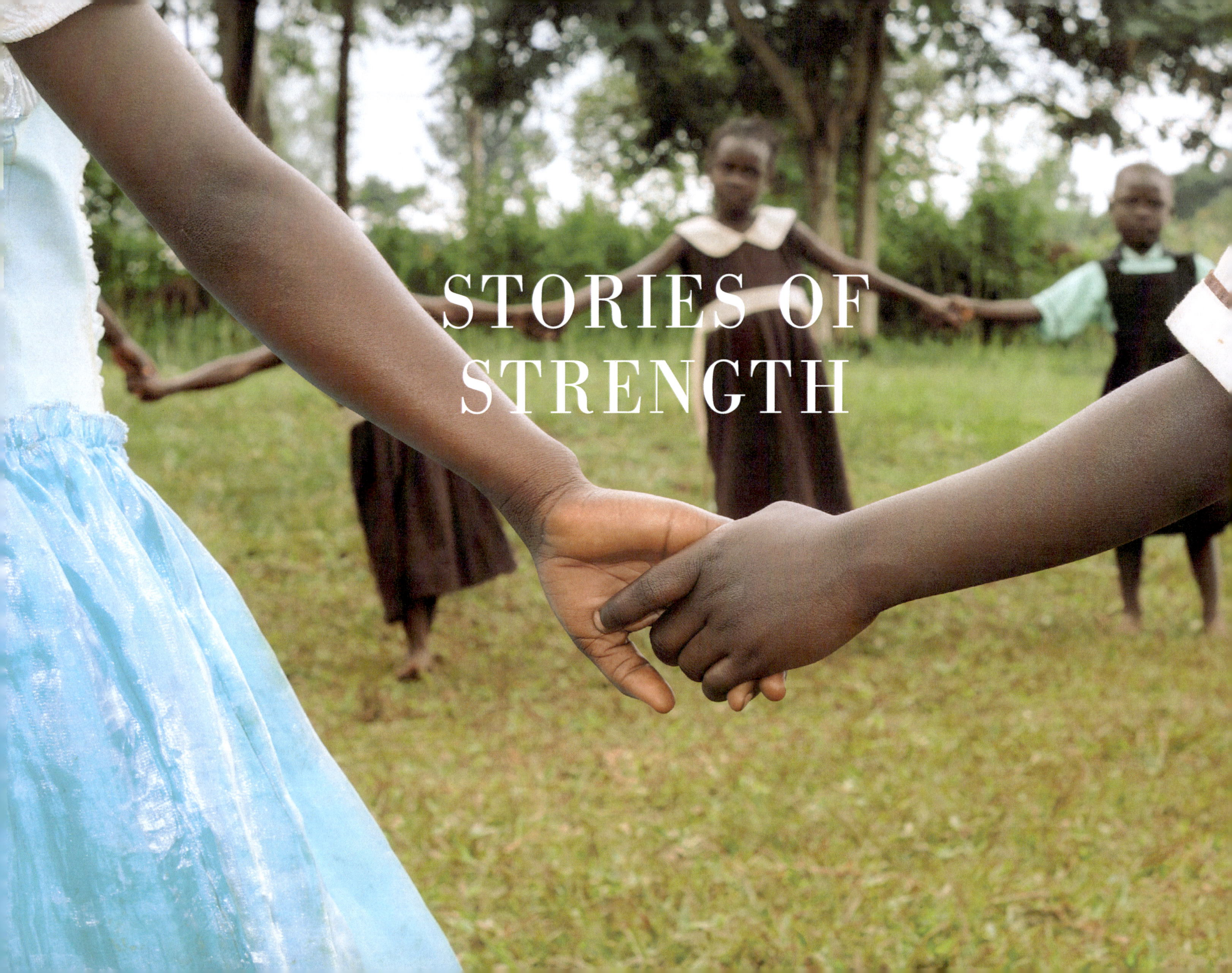
STORIES OF STRENGTH

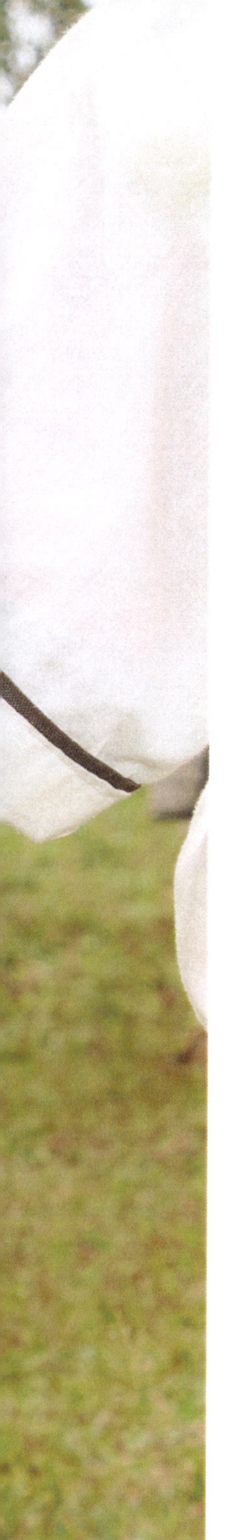

The Democratic Republic of Congo's eastern provinces have endured decades of conflict. Since 1996, over 6 million people have died in what the International Rescue Committee calls "the world's deadliest crisis." Armed groups fight for control of mineral resources such as cobalt for our smartphones, and coltan for our computers. Families flee when violence erupts, walking hundreds of miles to reach Uganda's borders.

Here, Uganda's progressive refugee policy offers something rare: the right to work, move freely, and access education. Yet survival remains a daily challenge.

In a world often marked by uncertainty, there are places where hope takes root like a living tree: quiet, steady, and strong. Among Uganda's orphans and refugee communities, perseverance is not something spoken of… it is lived.

It is carried in small hands reaching for tomorrow, in friendships woven across hardship, and in the fierce tenderness of those who choose to stand together rather than fall apart.

Strength blooms not from what is easy, but from what is shared: laughter amid loss, dreams amid displacement, and love where the world once offered none.

The evidence is found in teachers like Robert, who transforms a patch of earth into a beacon of learning. The courage is lived so that true courage is not the absence of fear, but the refusal to let fear have the final word.

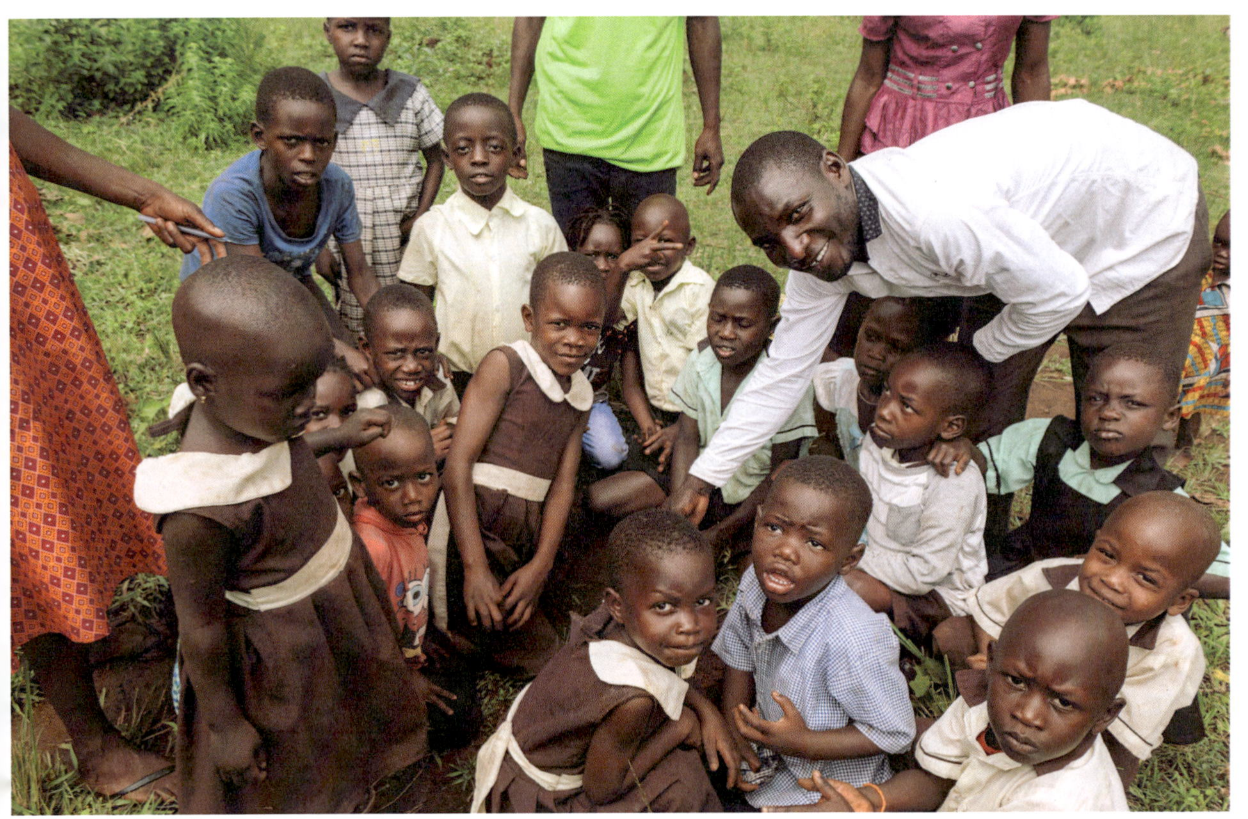

In the heart of Saviour Junior School, Director Wamani Robert leans into the circle of students he serves with unwavering hope.

His dreams for the school are vast: enough classrooms for every child, fair wages for teachers, and supplies to nourish education beyond survival.

Despite struggles to pay staff, buy basic materials, and protect lessons from leaking roofs, Robert's spirit remains unbroken.

His vision is clear—to build a true center of excellence in Masindi, where young minds are empowered to dream beyond their circumstances.

Through his leadership, he believes the next generation will transform their communities with creativity, innovation, and courage.

In the quiet strength of one small girl, we glimpse the hopes of an entire school.

She stands for the many students of Saviour Junior School—children like Ahebwa Edith, who dreams of becoming a teacher; Kayesu Cleopatra, who hopes to become a lawyer; and Talemwa Mario, who simply longs for a bright future.

Some are orphans, some walk from nearby villages, but all carry dreams bigger than the hardships they face.

Their hopes are stitched into every classroom, their determination into every lesson—a reminder that no child is ever too small to hold the weight of a dream.

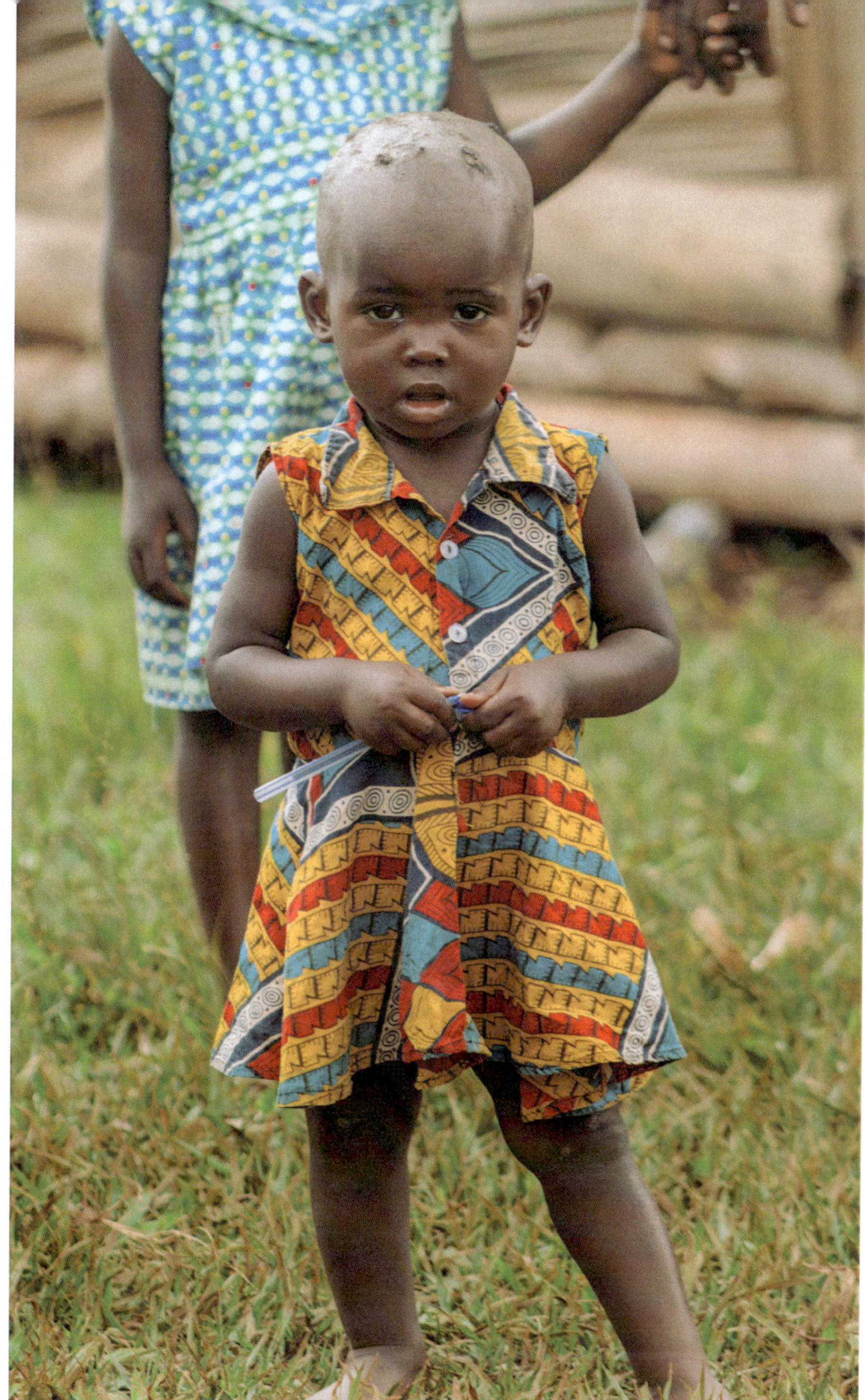

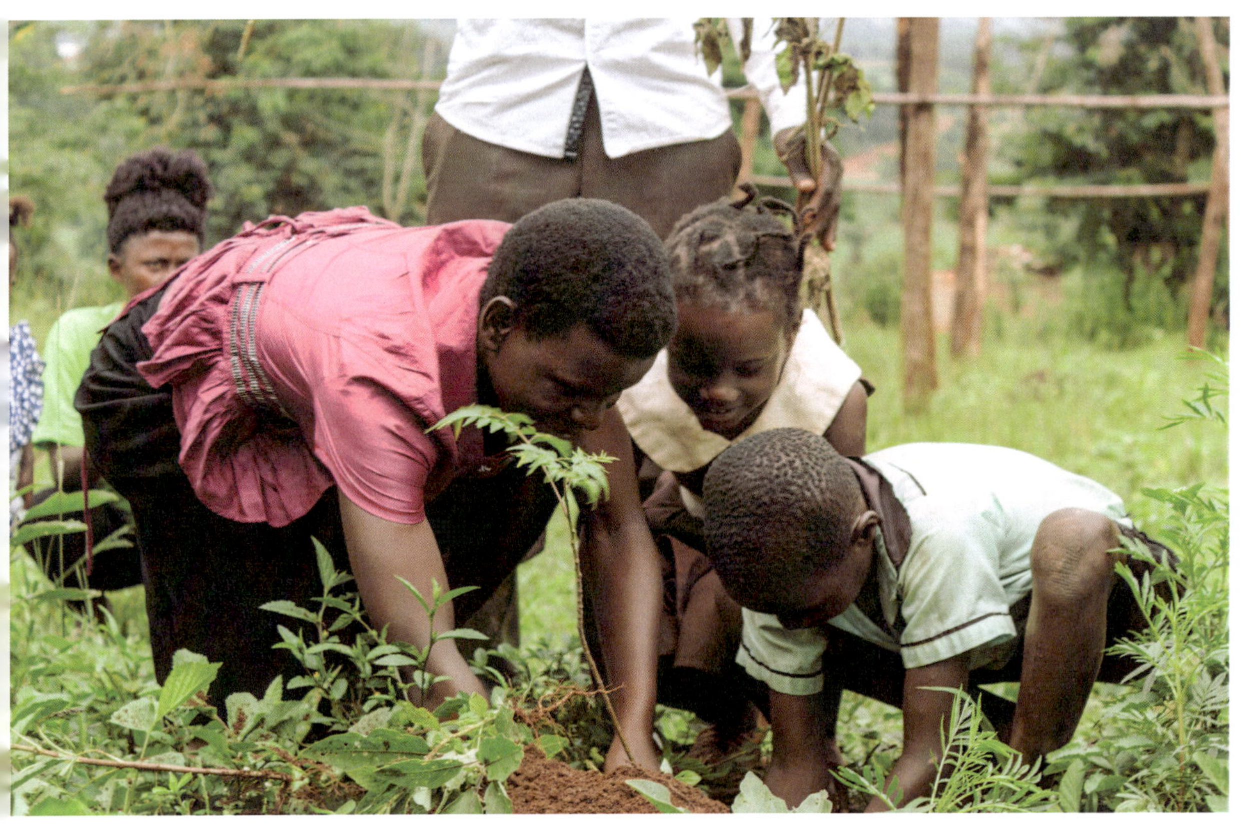

At Saviour Junior School, even the smallest hands plant seeds of hope.

Guided by their teachers, orphaned and vulnerable students press young roots into the earth—learning that healing, like growth, begins beneath the surface.

Each seedling is more than a lesson in agriculture; it is a declaration of belief in tomorrow.

In soil and sunlight, they claim their place in a world that has not always been gentle with them—and begin, quietly but powerfully, to grow upward.

In the warmth between a teacher and her students, the future quietly stirs.

The teachers of Saviour Junior School dream not just of more books, or sturdier classrooms—but of a world where every child learns without hunger, fear, or interruption.

Amid challenges like leaking roofs, shortages of teaching supplies, and the daily struggle to provide balanced meals, they stand steadfast—nurturing resilience one child at a time.

Their message to the world echoes through their work: invest in the hearts of children, and you invest in a future where hope will never run dry.

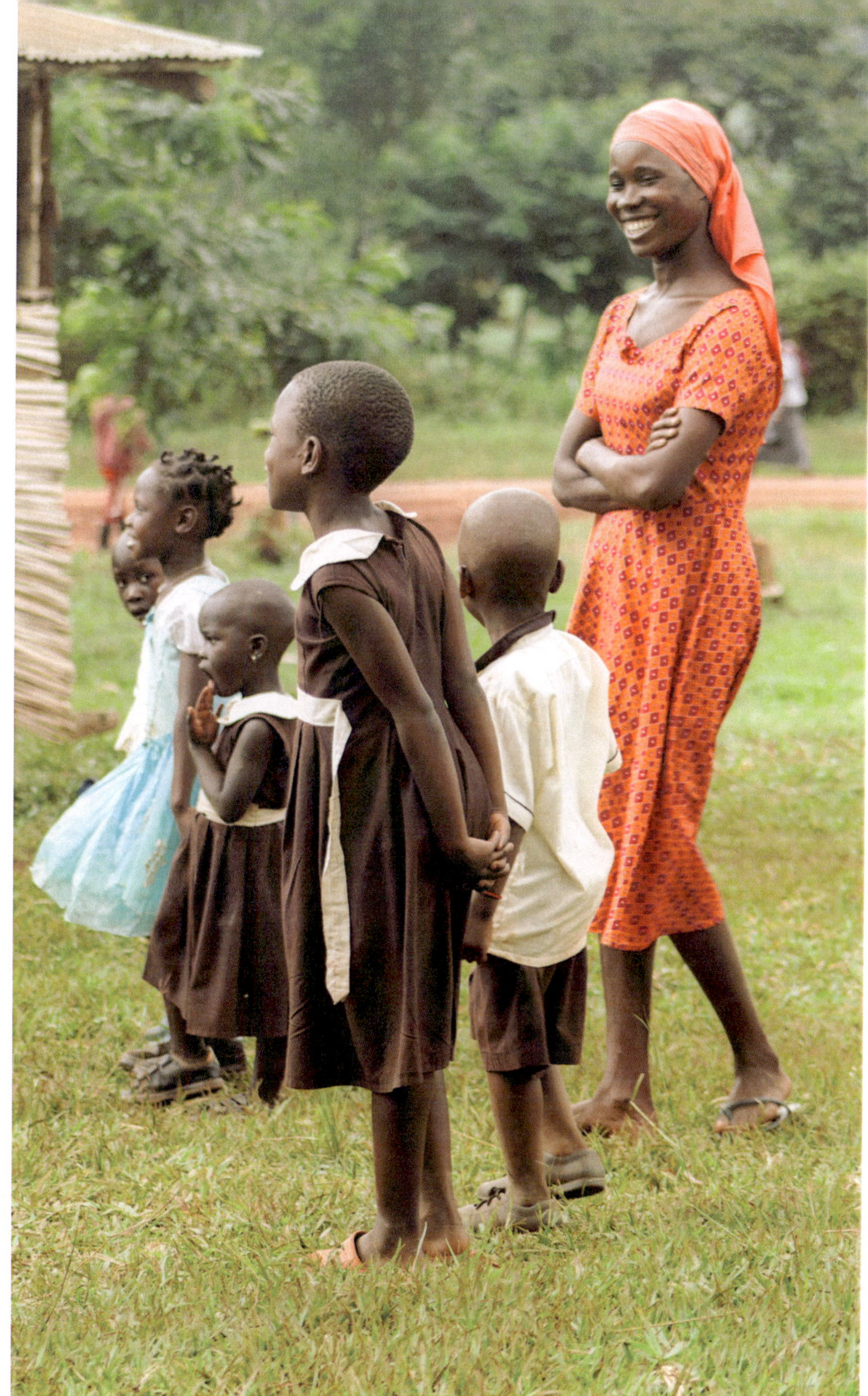

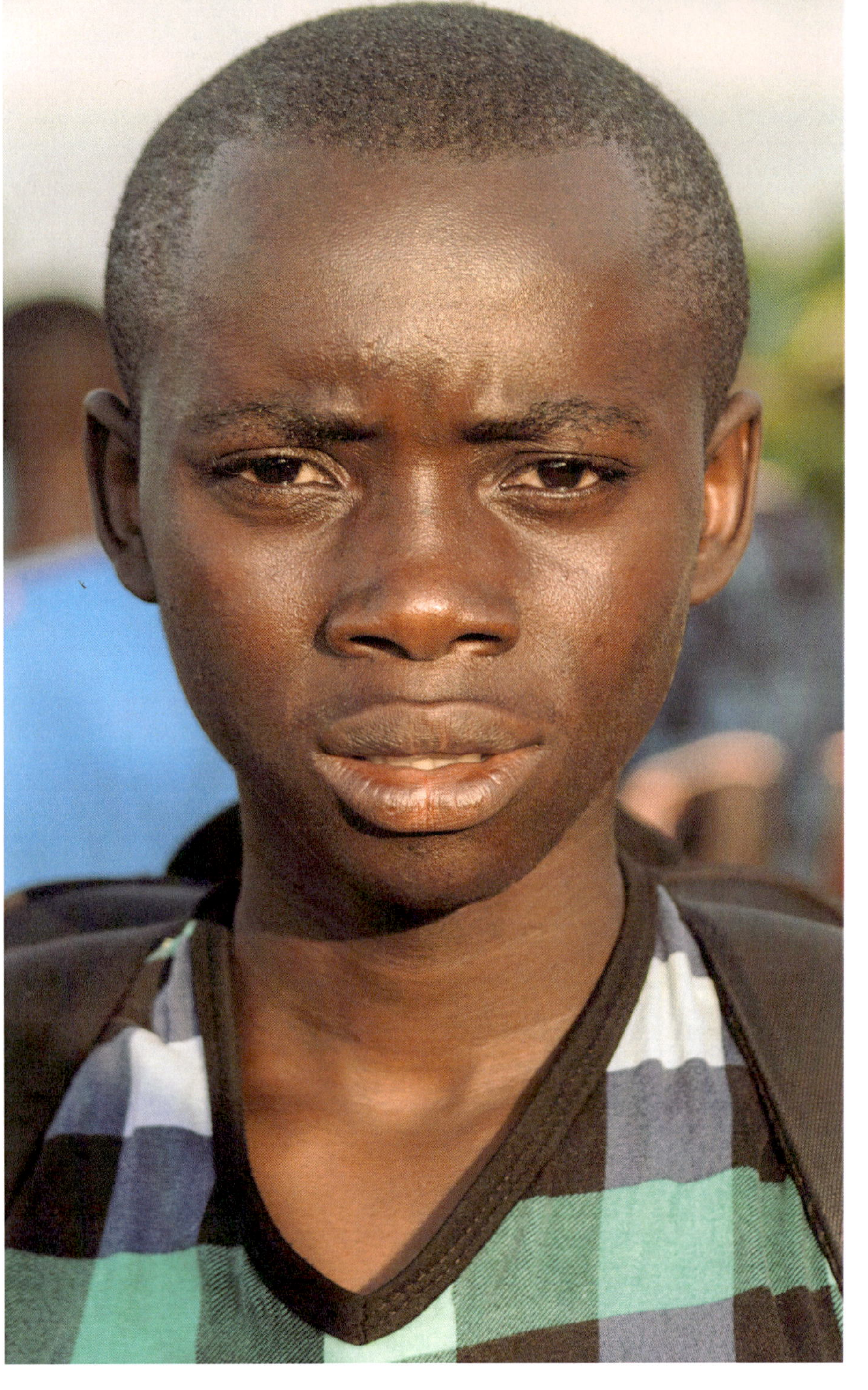

MUGISHA BENSON: DREAMING IN CODE

Captured two years ago at Kyangwali Refugee Settlement, this portrait of Mugisha Benson reveals the quiet determination of a young man on the rise. Born in the Democratic Republic of Congo and now 19 years old, Benson is a student at CIYOTA Secondary School in Uganda—a place he once feared he might never reach.

Through CIYOTA programs like *Education Cannot Wait*, he has overcome the weight of stress and uncertainty, embracing education not only as a lifeline, but as a launchpad. From computing to entrepreneurship and leadership training, Benson has gained the skills—and confidence—to pursue his dream.

"Since my childhood, I loved computing so much, and I will never go past computing and engineering."

"My dream is to become a great software engineer—and I know I will."

His journey is a living testament to the power of education, especially for refugee youth. In Benson's eyes lives a future built not on fear, but on purpose.

SPREADING LOVE, NOT WAR

Nadia and Joshua stand side by side at Kyangwali Refugee Settlement, their smiles radiant, their stories woven with resilience.

Nadia—also known as *Beauty Queen Buari*—was born in Goma, DRC, and raised as the eldest of eight siblings. Her dream of becoming a fashion designer is stitched with creativity, spiritual faith, and the will to rise beyond hardship.

> *"Personal growth gives me hope… I think I have to go forward, not backward, until I achieve my dreams."*

Joshua, born in Bunia, Ituri Province, came to Kyangwali at the age of three and has been part of CIYOTA for nearly a decade. Through years of displacement and uncertainty, he found strength in education and purpose in justice. He hopes to become a lawyer and fight the injustices that fractured his homeland.

> *"Keep grinding always because nobody cares—not until you make it."*

Together, they represent a generation of young refugees determined to rewrite their futures—with dignity, vision, and unshakable hope.

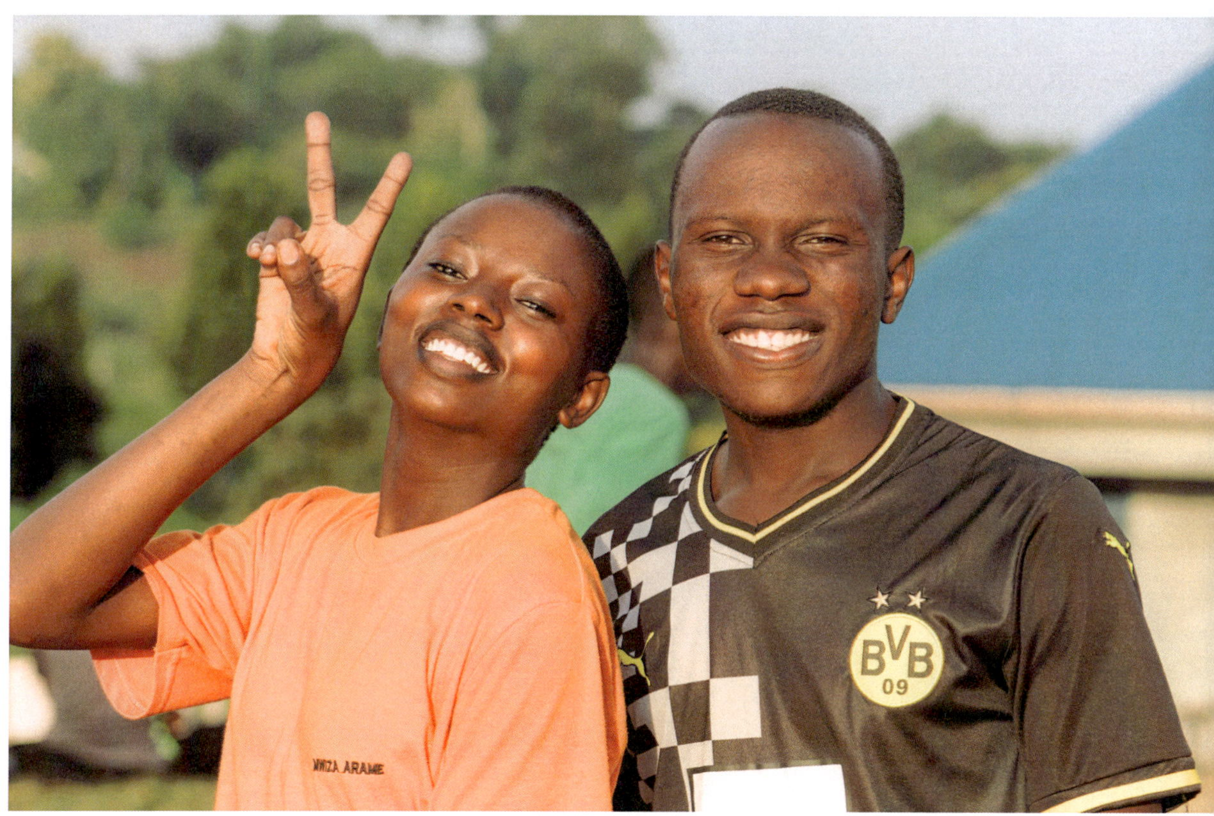

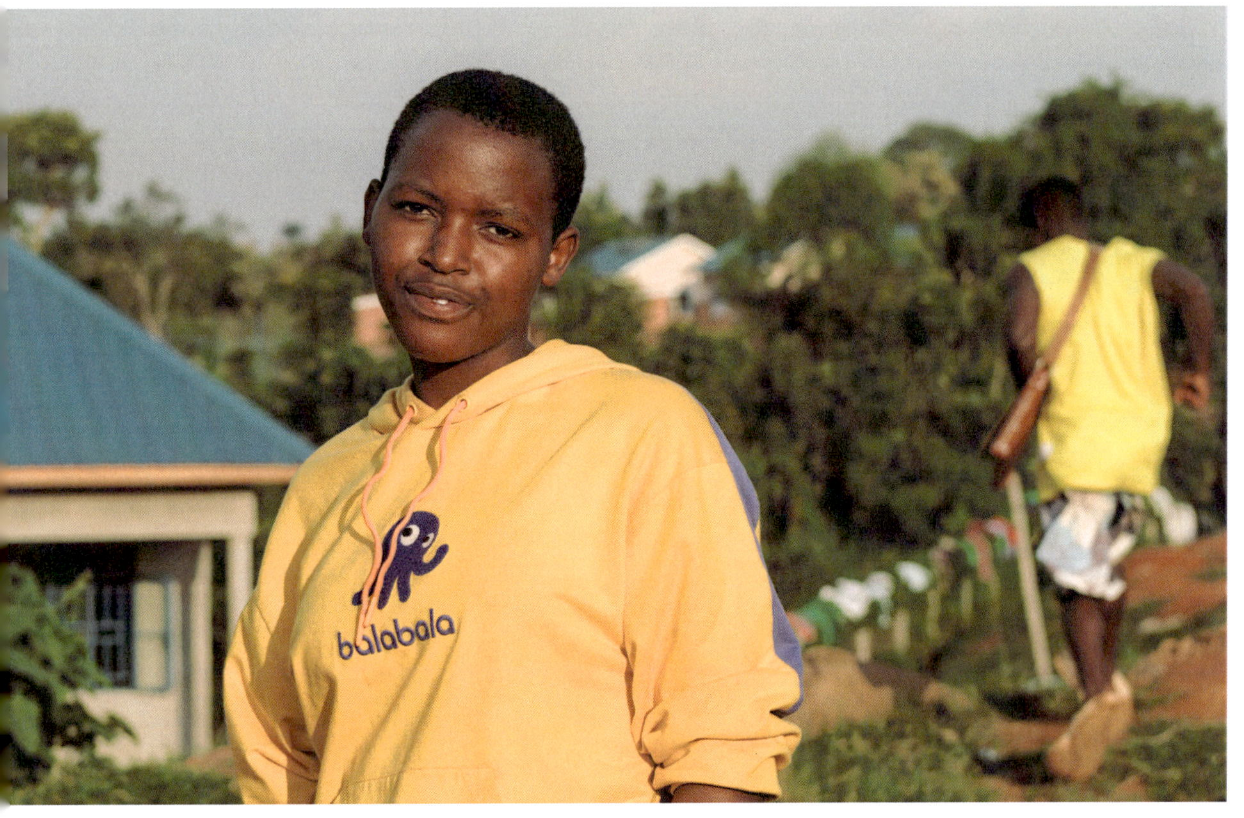

HOPE IN THE MIDST OF HARDSHIP

Uwamahoro Alice stands with quiet determination at Kyangwali Refugee Settlement, her journey marked by courage far beyond her years. Born in the Democratic Republic of Congo, she fled political instability with her family and sought refuge in Uganda. In a community where girl child education was seen as wasteful and marriage was expected, Alice chose a different path, one paved with perseverance.

To pay her own school fees, she began hairdressing as a child, juggling business and studies while battling societal norms. Even when pressured to marry to help cover her father's medical bills, she held onto her dreams.

Joining CIYOTA Secondary School in 2022 marked a turning point. Through the mentorship of CIYOTA staff like Elosha Kapata and the sanctuary of education, Alice began to heal, rebuild her confidence, and rekindle her aspirations.

Now pursuing computer science, Alice is determined to become a voice for girls and refugees, proving that education represents far more than a right but serves as a revolution.

"Ladies can also contribute to the economy of a community and a country at large… Success is a process, not a day one achievement."

THE ONES WE MISS

She knelt with pride, a basketball resting beneath her palms, her eyes lit with hope and possibility. A refugee student at Kyangwali Refugee Settlement, she radiated joy the day we met—her spirit vibrant, her laughter contagious. But today, she is no longer in school.

Her absence is a quiet ache felt across the landscape of opportunity.

Many refugee girls face immense barriers to education: poverty, early marriage, gender discrimination, trauma, and the heavy burden of domestic responsibilities. In Uganda, even with incredible efforts by organizations like CIYOTA and dedicated educators, dropout rates remain high—especially among adolescent girls. Each student lost is a story unfinished, a dream deferred.

This image is a reminder: behind every dropout statistic is a soul full of life, a young mind that once dared to dream. Her smile is not forgotten. It is a call to action—to build systems that catch those on the edge, to ensure that all children, especially girls, can stay in school and thrive.

Because no one should disappear from the promise of a better tomorrow.

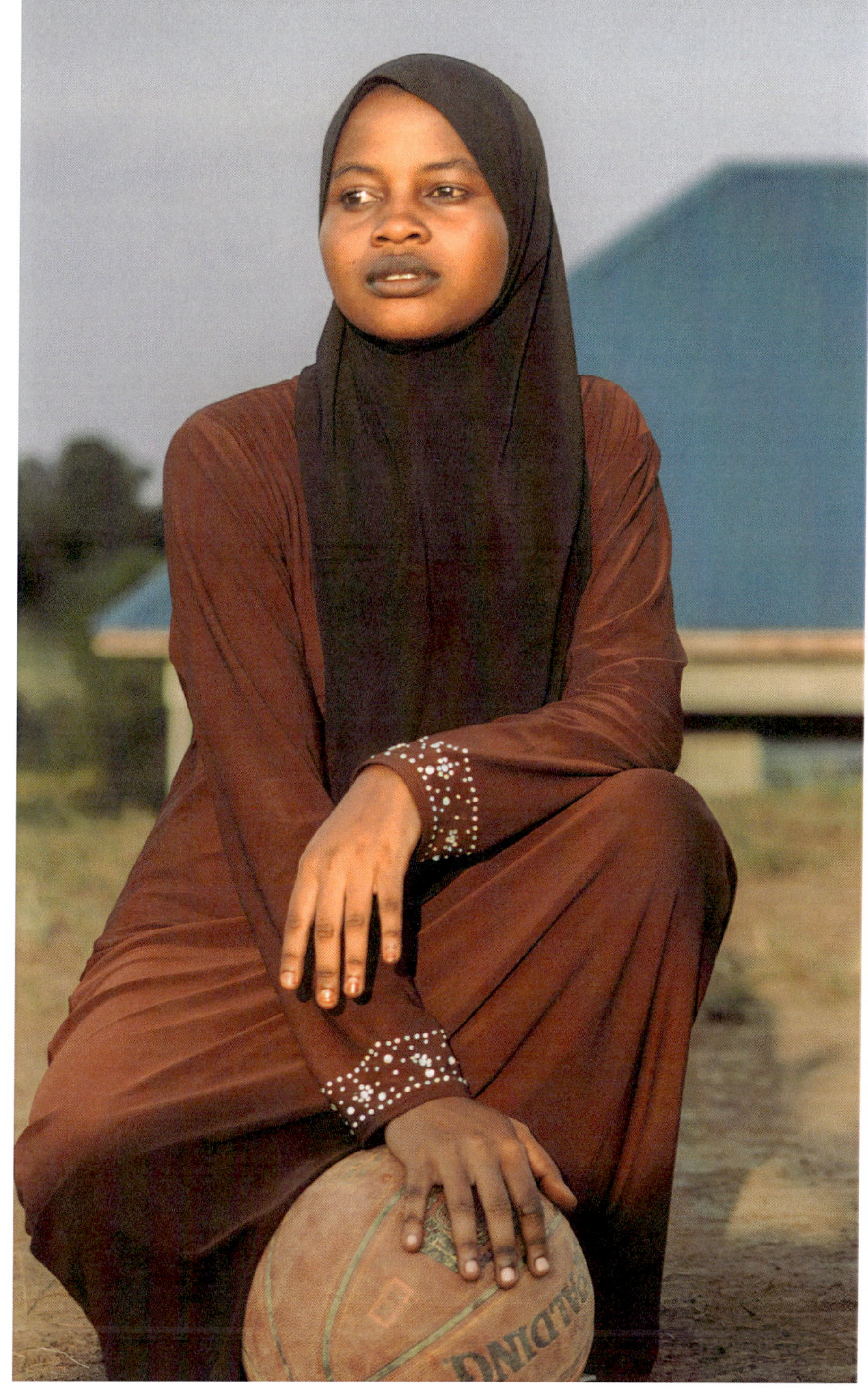

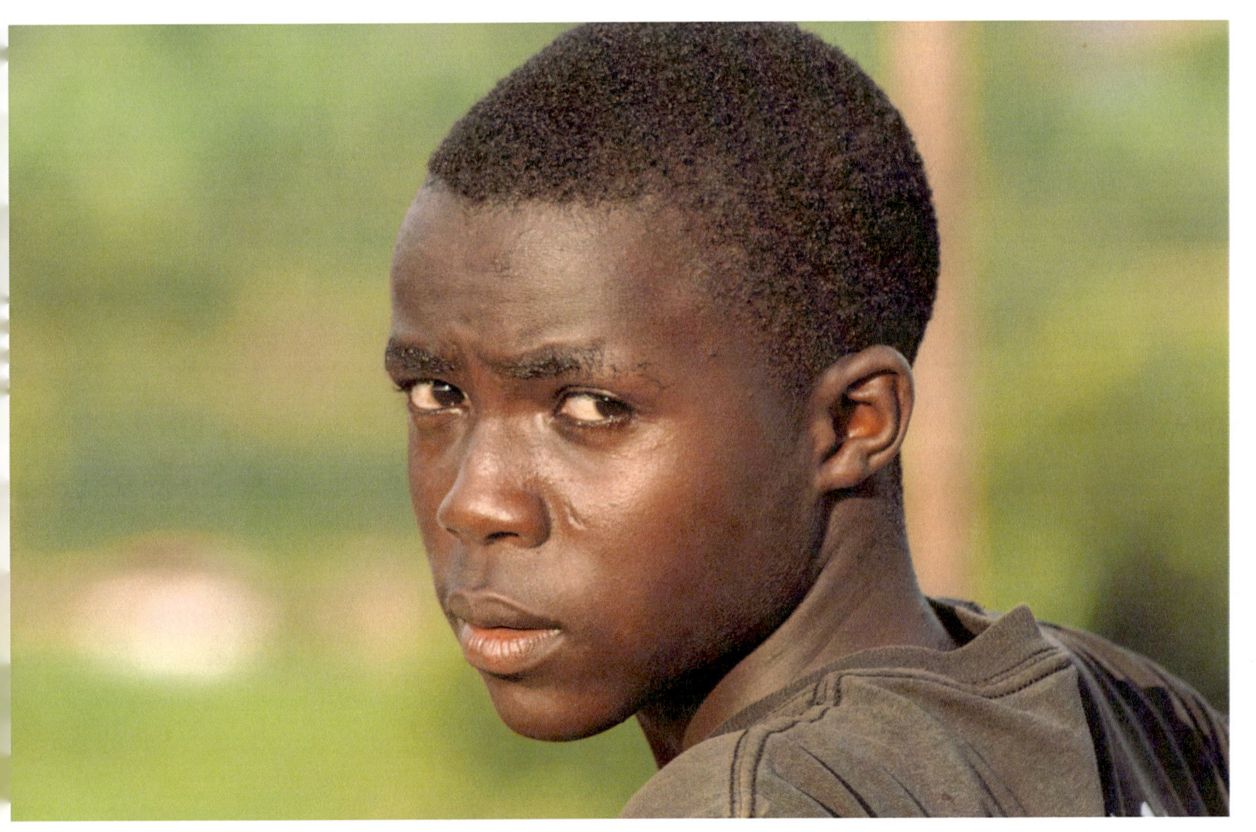

THE JOURNEY BEYOND

His gaze holds a thousand unspoken stories—of endurance, of displacement, of quiet strength shaped by the soil of Kyangwali Refugee Settlement. When this photo was taken, he stood on Ugandan ground. Today, he walks another path across the ocean, having immigrated to the United States.

We never got to hear his full story. But his presence—anchored in that golden afternoon light—reminds us that stories of strength do not always end where they begin. For many refugee youth, education and support open doors to new continents, new lives. And yet, even as they move forward, their roots remain—deep in the red earth, in the friendships forged under sun and hardship.

In the quiet power of his stare, we witness both where he came from and all that is yet to come.

LEGEND OF THE STREETS

When war swept through his village in eastern Congo, Joshua was just eleven. He returned home from school to find his parents gone, his house empty, and his world changed. For an entire year, he and his younger siblings—two brothers and a baby sister—survived alone. They slept in abandoned buildings, begged strangers for food, and once lived for a week on nothing but chewed sorghum and water. "We became the Legends of the Streets," he writes.

Though surrounded by hardship, Joshua never stopped going to school. He repeated Primary 6 four times before CIYOTA found him, welcomed him, and helped him begin again. "CIYOTA is the Hope of the Hopeless," he writes. Support from a sponsor in North Carolina—whom he now calls "Mom"—covered his school fees and gave him the encouragement he needed to keep going.

Now in secondary school, Joshua dreams of becoming a leader who inspires others.

"Do your best in everything. Support if you can, because what you call small may turn someone's pages to white—and help them start a new chapter."

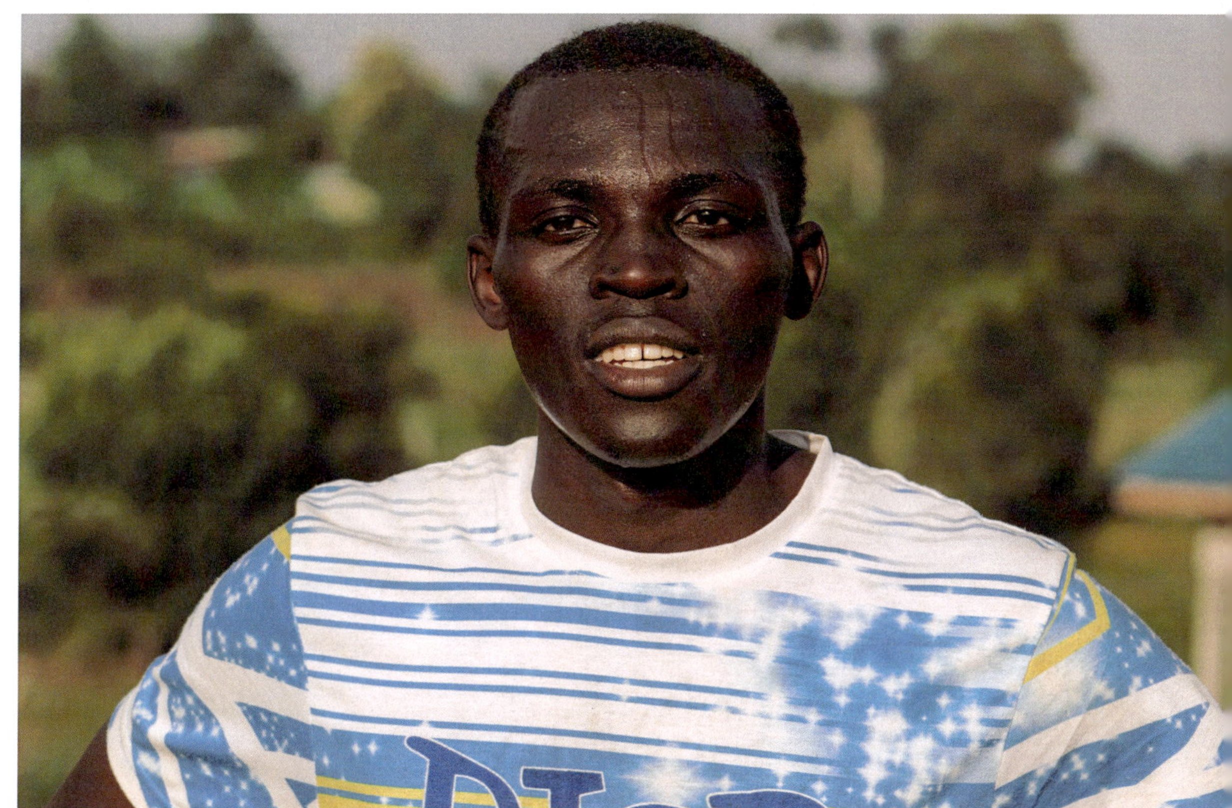

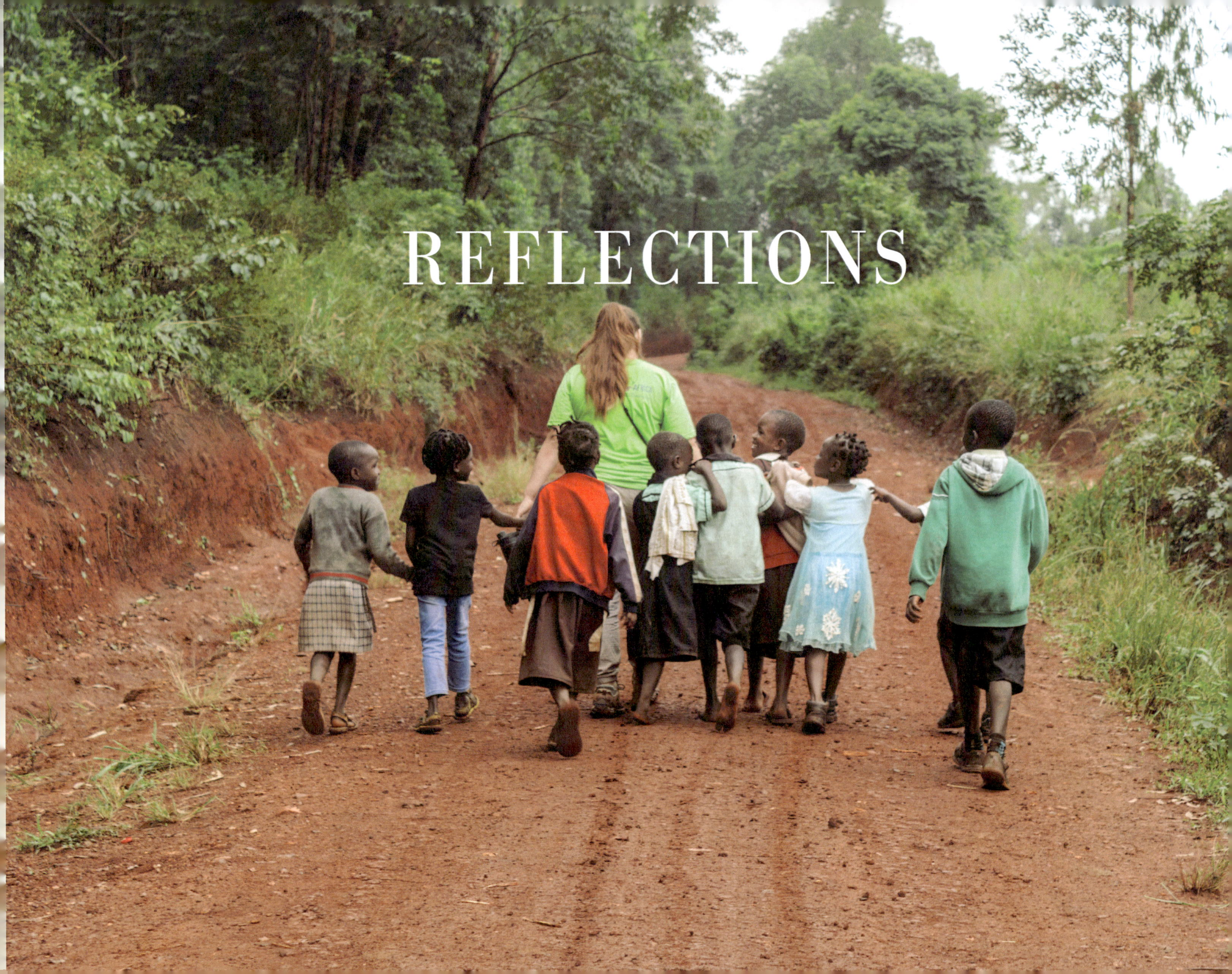
REFLECTIONS

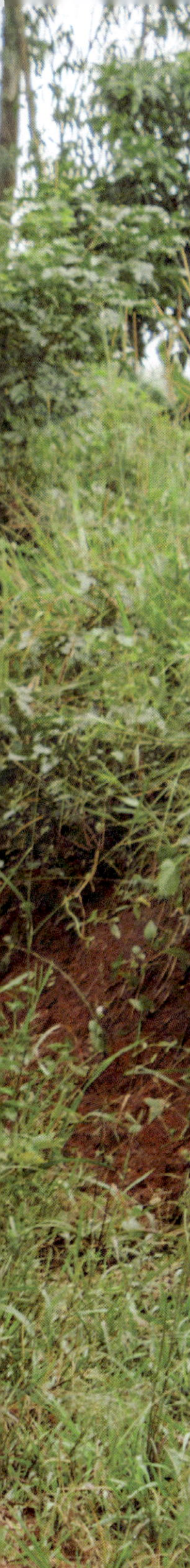

Standing on Ugandan soil, I could feel the weight of proximity—knowing that just across the border, families were still fleeing the violence we'd read about in headlines. The Democratic Republic of Congo felt impossibly close, its pain almost tangible in the stories carried by those who had walked hundreds of miles to safety.

Yet here, in the green embrace of Uganda's refugee settlements, I witnessed something that challenged everything I thought I knew about displacement and despair. Children who had lost everything were learning to dream again. Mothers who had fled with nothing were building new communities. Young men like Joshua were transforming their trauma into purpose.

My daughter and I came to Uganda thinking we would give something—time, resources, hope. Instead, we found ourselves receiving lessons in resilience that no classroom could teach. At Saviour Junior School, watching Lena connect instantly with Ugandan orphans and the children of my colleagues, seeing how quickly barriers dissolved in shared play and laughter, we discovered that healing happens in relationship. In the patient way Cleofash later taught her to prepare traditional meals, in the quiet strength of Alice as she pursued her education against all odds, we learned that hope takes many forms.

This is why I chose to support Agri Planet Africa: Not because they offered easy solutions to complex problems, but because they understood something profound: that nurturing the future means investing in people, not just programs. In a region where conflict has stolen so many childhoods, they were quietly creating spaces where dreams could take root again.

These images capture more than moments. They reveal the extraordinary power of ordinary connections. In a world that often feels fractured, here was proof that love grows fastest where it is freely given, and hope is most powerful when shared.

The contrast still moves me: so close to ongoing conflict, yet here we witnessed the daily miracle of people choosing to build rather than destroy, to welcome rather than fear, to plant seeds of possibility in soil that others might see as barren.

This is the gift Uganda gave us, the understanding that resilience is not built in isolation, but nurtured across generations, passed from heart to heart like a living flame of hope.

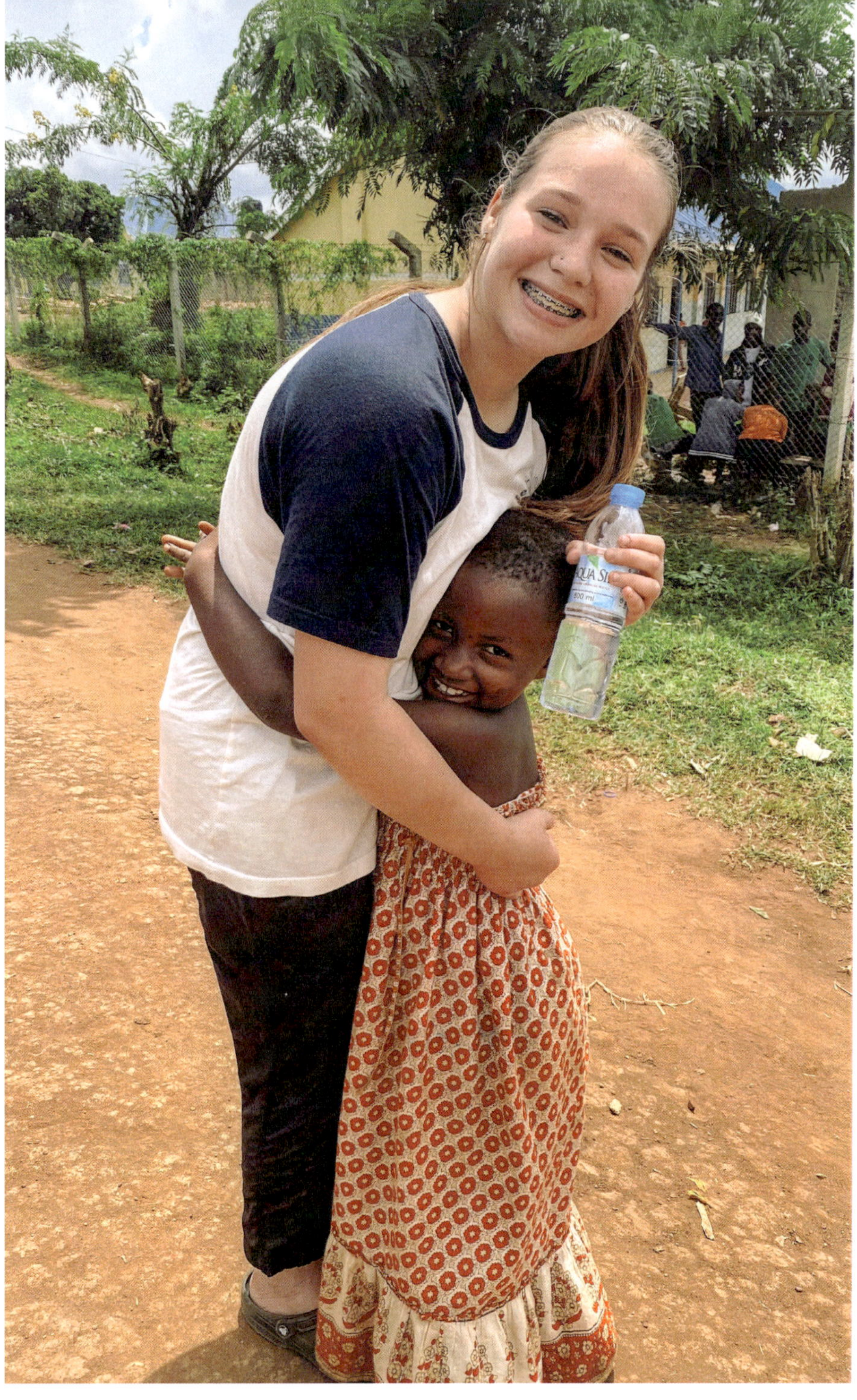

In a spontaneous moment of joy, a young girl ran up and wrapped her arms around Lena, holding tight as if they'd known each other forever. On this red-dirt path through Kyangwali, no words were needed—just the language of love and open hearts.

After an afternoon of agricultural training at Agri Planet Africa's headquarters, we returned to find Lena surrounded by the students of Saviour Junior School.

The children had raced back ahead of us, eager and full of laughter, gathering around Lena as if to hold onto the spirit of connection she had sparked in them.

In that circle of small hands and bright eyes, the true heart of resilience was clear: love grows fastest where it is freely given.

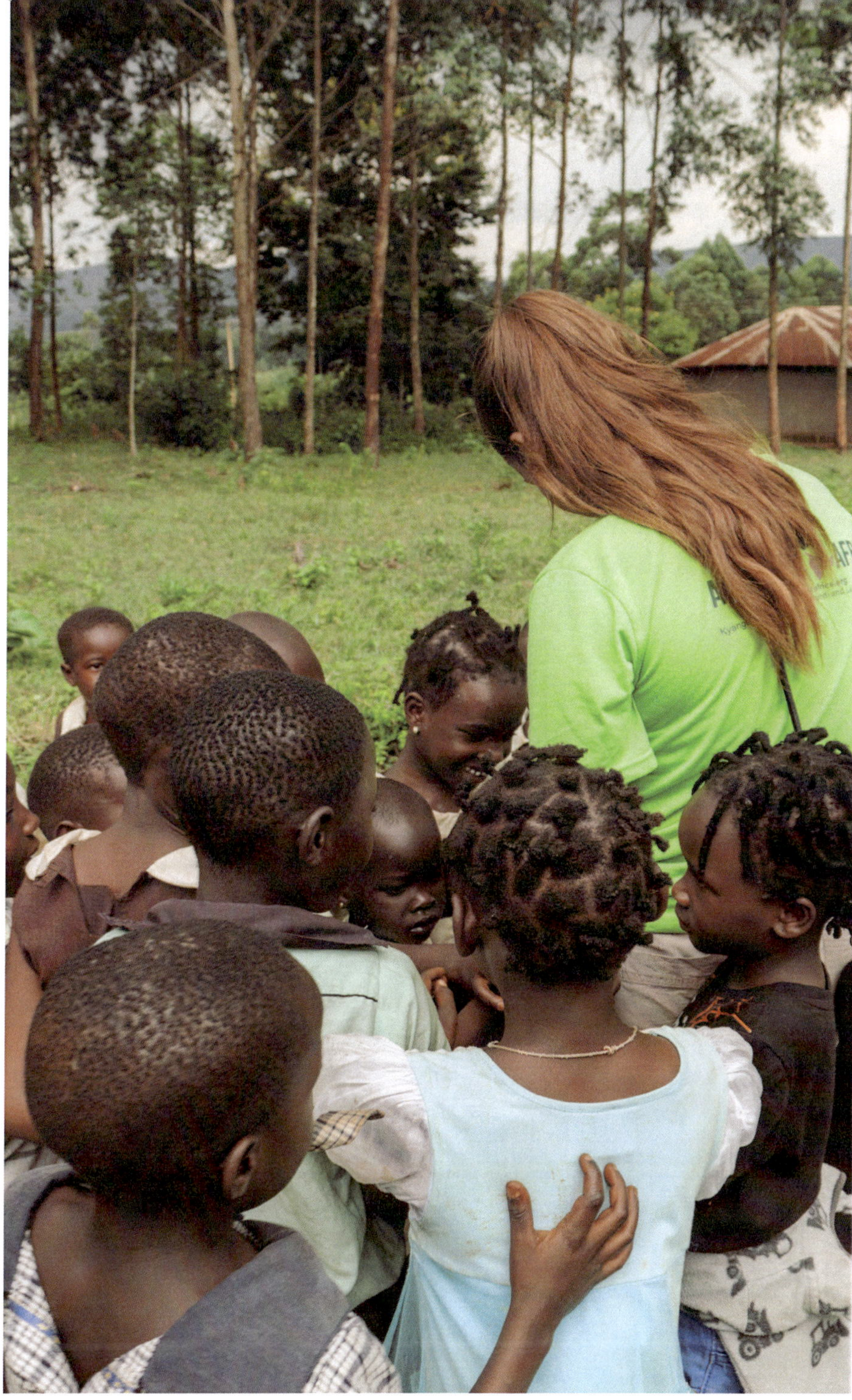

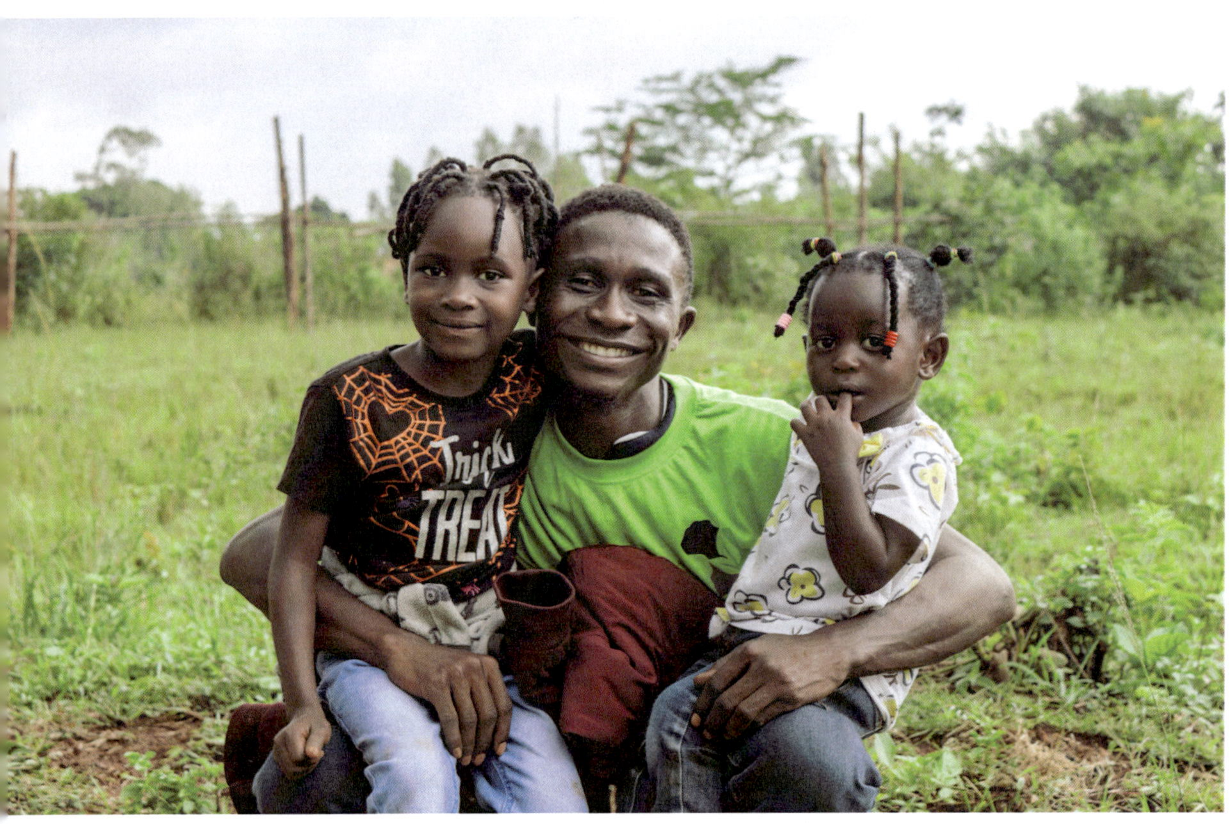

Seated quietly in the green embrace of Uganda's fields, Cleofash holds his two daughters — Kaganzi Keron (*Amooti*) and Kunihira Anastatious (*Abwooli*) — with a father's steady pride. Keron, the elder, dreams of one day becoming an entertainer, her spirit already carrying a spark for the future. Little Anastatious, still cradled in innocence, holds the sweetness of new beginnings.

In the tenderness between them, we glimpse the deeper truth: resilience is not built in a moment — it is nurtured across generations, passed from heart to heart like a living flame of hope.

Wrapped in a moment of pure trust, Lena cradles baby Janelle, a living symbol of Agri Planet Africa's hopes for the next generation. In a field stitched with connection, two worlds meet under one green promise: to nurture, to empower, and to grow.

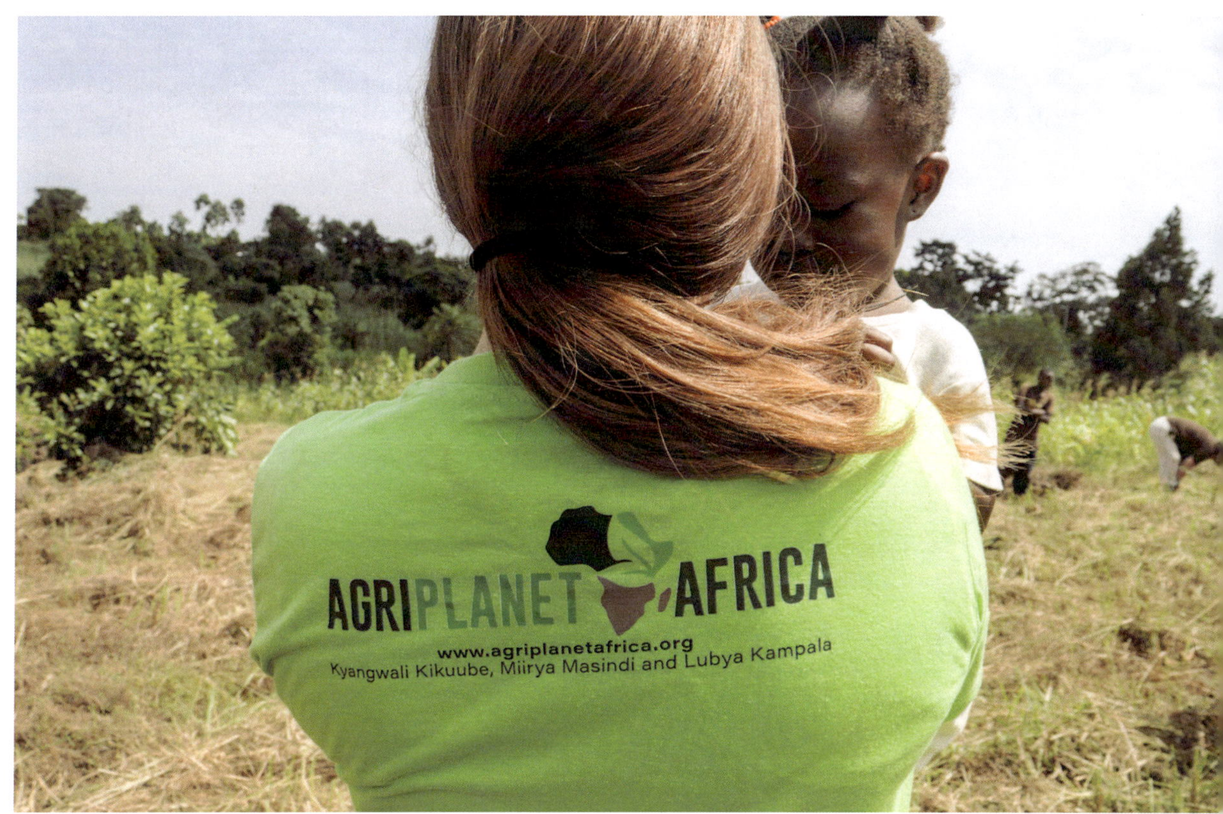

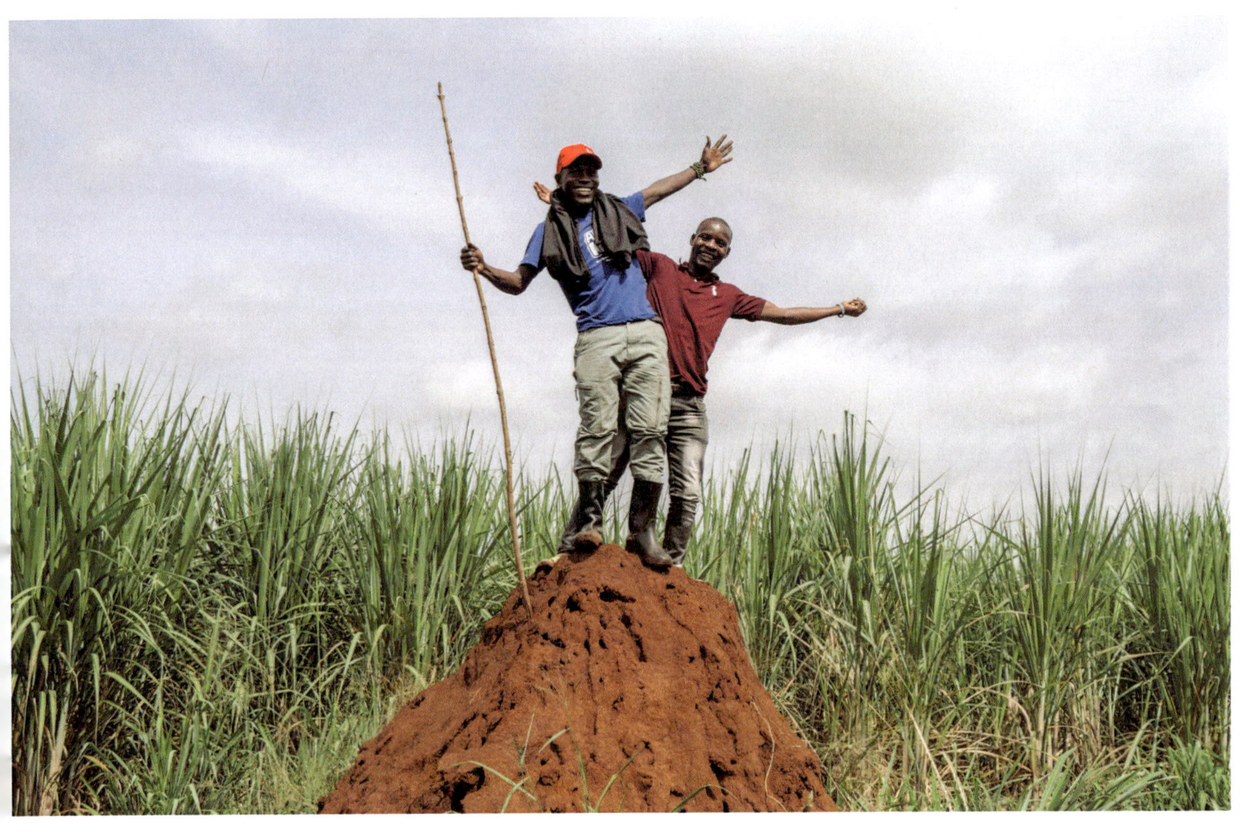

Ignatius and Brian stand triumphantly atop a towering termite mound — a natural monument to the power of patience, persistence, and collective effort.
In Uganda's fields of strength, even the smallest hands can build mighty things.

Lena and Jackie (*Akiiki*), sister to Cleofash and Ignatius, share a meal in the family's home where Cleofash and Ignatius spent their childhood. Within these walls, generations have gathered in love and hospitality, the same spirit now shared with new friends from across the world.

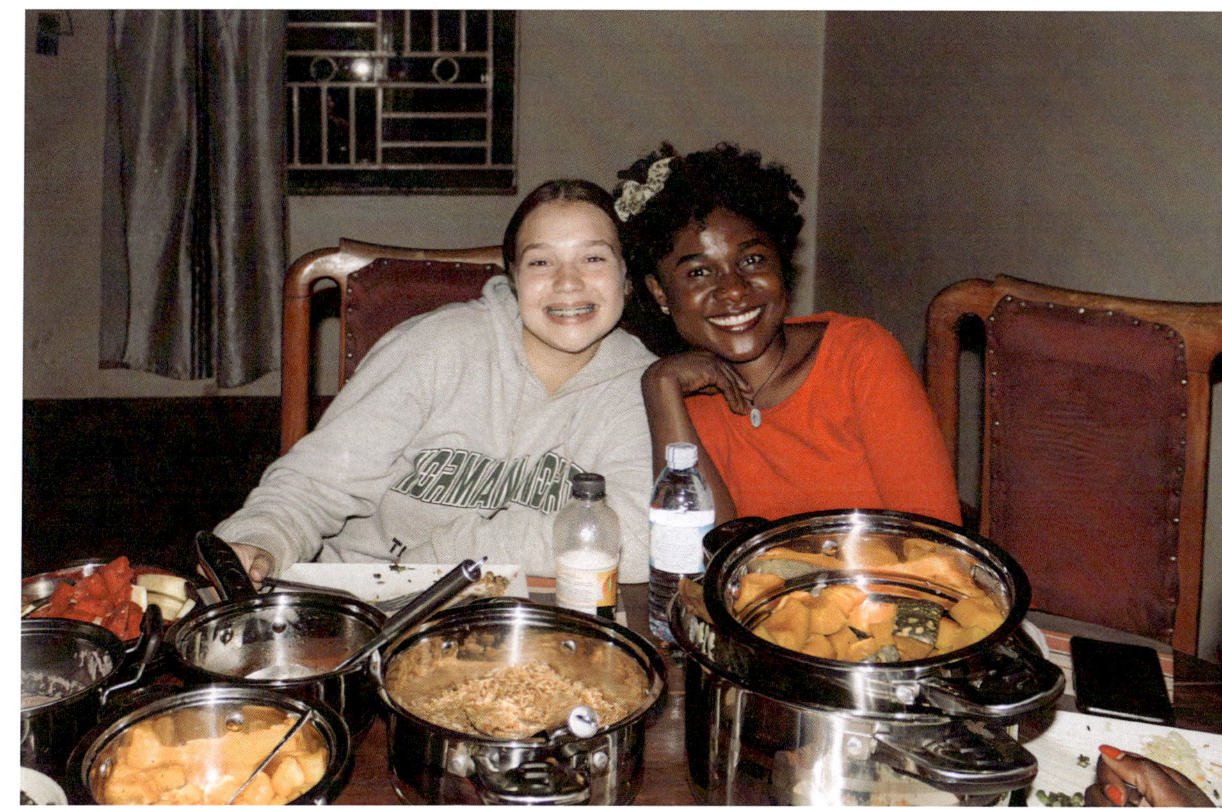

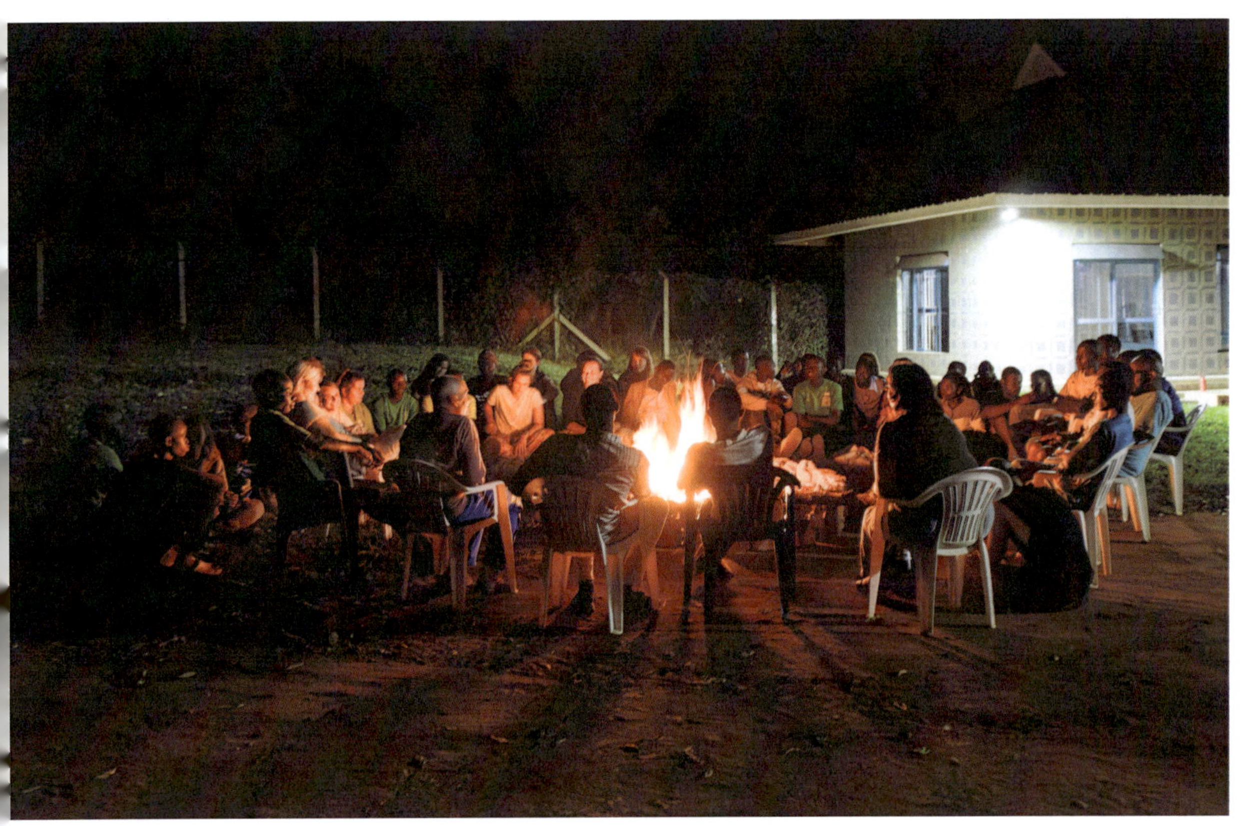

On our final night at Kyangwali Refugee Settlement, we gathered around a fire built with our own hands—volunteers from Love Africa Mission, students and staff from CIYOTA, and our small team woven together by purpose, not chance.

Beneath a sky strewn with stars, the fire's soft glow became more than warmth—it became a torch passed between hearts.

Stories were shared, laughter rose like sparks into the night, and silent promises flickered in the embers:

To carry hope forward.

To build beyond borders.

To keep the flame of resilience alive, wherever life leads us.

The Journey Continues

In every seed planted, every hand held, and every story shared, we found the same truth: strength grows not from what we possess, but from what we share. Strength is not born from despair, love blooms, from the fierce tenderness of communities who refuse to abandon each other.

Uganda taught us that abundance isn't measured in bank accounts but in bonds between neighbors, in wisdom passed through generations, in the patient tending of what matters most. Fields of Resilience is not just a journey through Uganda, it is a tribute to the resolve that unites us all, a testament to what we create when we choose connection over distance, hope over despair, and community over isolation.

The trees we planted will outlive us all. The children we met will become leaders. The farmers will feed their families for generations. This is how change happens—not through grand gestures, but through the quiet revolutionaries who tend their communities with unwavering devotion.

Though this chapter closes, the stories do not. They live on: in the trees taking root, in the hands that will harvest, and in every heart willing to listen. Thank you for walking this path with us.

What you can do:
- *Support Agri Planet Africa at agriplanetafrica.org. Volunteer with organizations in your own community.*
- *Practice sustainable farming.*
- *Share this story.*
- *Most importantly, look for the quiet revolutionaries in your own neighborhood, and join them.*

May you leave these pages carrying new seeds of compassion, ready to plant them wherever you go.

Acknowledgments

To the communities of Uganda — thank you for welcoming me with open arms and hearts. Your resilience, kindness, and strength are the soul of this book. You showed me that true beauty lies in connection, not comfort.

To Agri Planet Africa — especially Ahumuza Ignatius (*Ateenyi*), Alinaitwe Cleofash (*Atwooki*), and Dr. Byarugaba Benjamin (*Atwooki*) — your vision of empowerment and sustainability inspired every page. Thank you for trusting me to help share your story with the world.

To Ahumuza Janelle Africa (*Akiiki*) — it is one of the greatest honors of my life to share a name with you. May your life bloom with the same hope and resilience this book seeks to honor.

To my daughter, Lena — your courage in traveling halfway across the world with me, your laughter with the children at Kyangwali Refugee Settlement, and your willingness to embrace every moment with an open heart — you are a living testament to resilience and compassion.

To Alex, my husband — thank you for your unwavering support, your belief in my dreams, and your patience during the many long days and nights of writing, editing, and reflection. You are my home.

To my parents — thank you for celebrating my love of learning and exploration, and for encouraging me to follow my heart wherever it led.

To my Aunt, Dr. Lois Nightingale — your encouragement and the light you bring into the world have touched my heart more than words can say. Thank you for inspiring me to keep reaching, learning, and believing.

To the Saviour Junior School community and the children of Kyangwali Refugee Settlement — your faces, your stories, your smiles in the face of hardship — you are not forgotten. This book is a promise to you: that your resilience matters.

To Buddha Mind Monastery and Grand Master Wei Chueh — your teachings on compassion, mindfulness, and the interconnectedness of all beings shaped how I walked this journey.

To Grandma VeVe — your love crossed oceans and generations. Your words still ground me: "Nothing is constant save change." May I carry your light, as you once carried mine.

To the global community of friends, mentors, and colleagues who encouraged this dream — thank you for reminding me that storytelling has the power to spark change, even when the road feels steep.

And finally, to my inner child — who once feared her voice didn't matter — may you always know: your stories are your strength, and your dreams are the seeds of resilience you plant in the world.

With heart and gratitude,

Janelle

Janelle Nightingale is a global storyteller, nonprofit leader, and lifelong advocate for resilience, education, and compassion.

With a background in strategic communication and digital strategy, Janelle has dedicated her career to helping organizations amplify their missions and connect hearts across cultures.

As Executive Director of Agri Planet Africa, she traveled to Uganda to support sustainable agriculture initiatives, leadership development, and education projects. What she found there was more than a mission—it was a second home.

Janelle's work is rooted in the belief that stories have the power to heal, connect, and ignite change. Through her writing and photography, she seeks to honor the quiet courage of communities rising in strength and unity, often against unimaginable odds.

A practicing Buddhist, passionate traveler, and advocate for global connection, Janelle holds a master's degree in strategic communication and digital strategy. She believes that every story planted with care can bloom into resilience—and that even in the most unexpected places, hope takes root.

Fields of Resilience is her tribute to the extraordinary spirit of Uganda—and to the unbreakable threads of humanity that bind us all.

**We are all connected by the seeds we plant
and the stories we share.**

— JANELLE NIGHTINGALE (*AKIIKI*)

About Agri Planet Africa

Agri Planet Africa is a nonprofit organization dedicated to cultivating sustainable agriculture, education, and leadership across Uganda and beyond. Founded by Ahumuza Ignatius and Alinaitwe Cleofash, two visionary leaders deeply rooted in their communities, Agri Planet Africa empowers individuals and families to transform their futures through the land beneath their feet.

From establishing permaculture resource centers to offering agricultural training, seed bank programs, and mentorship opportunities, Agri Planet Africa provides the tools, knowledge, and support rural communities need to thrive. Their work encompasses far more than growing crops as it focuses on growing resilience, self-sufficiency, and hope.

At the heart of Agri Planet Africa is a systems-thinking approach. The organization addresses a dynamic network of evolving community needs including education, food security, leadership, and environmental stewardship through an adaptive model of grassroots innovation. Their efforts embody what scholars describe as a "reorganizing business model," one that succeeds not by narrowly defined outputs but by creating enabling conditions where local ingenuity, care, and collaboration can flourish.

One notable example is their mushroom cultivation initiative. Originally launched to support food security and income for orphanages during the COVID-19 pandemic, the project shifted when supply chains broke down. Rather than abandon the effort, one orphanage used the experience to reimagine its future by transitioning from dependency to sustainability by cultivating maize and engaging children in hands-on agricultural learning. This evolution was supported by the Evolutionary Funding Collaborative, a nontraditional funder that prioritizes contextual action learning over rigid deliverables. In this framework, the value lies not in guaranteed outcomes, but in emergent insight, shared learning, and system-level transformation.

This philosophy is woven through every branch of Agri Planet Africa's work. They don't simply teach permaculture but supply seeds, demonstrate techniques, help farmers reach markets, and challenge cultural stigmas around agriculture. Their impact is layered, long-term, and deeply embedded in community well-being.

80% of the proceeds from Fields of Resilience directly support Agri Planet Africa through Agri Planet Foundation, Inc., a 501(c)(3) nonprofit that facilitates U.S. donations to fund Agri Planet Africa's sustainable agriculture education, youth leadership training, and community resilience programs.

Learn more at **agriplanetfoundation.org**.

Credits

Photography
All photos captured by Janelle Nightingale unless otherwise noted.
With heartfelt gratitude to the communities of Uganda for graciously allowing their lives, stories, and landscapes to be shared with the world.

Contributors
- Ahumuza Ignatius (*Ateenyi*) – CEO, Agri Planet Africa
- Alinaitwe Cleofash (*Atwooki*) – Director of Innovations & Extension, Agri Planet Africa
- Ahaisibwe Brian (*Atwooki*) – Volunteer, Agri Planet Africa
- Komujuni Allen Shanita (*Akiiki*) – Community Leader and Agri Planet Africa Supporter
- The students and staff of Saviour Junior Primary School

Schools and Orphanages
- The residents of Kyangwali Refugee Settlement
- The students of CIYOTA (COBURWAS International Youth Organization to Transform Africa)

Support and Guidance
- **Agri Planet Africa** – For your unwavering collaboration and visionary leadership
- **Evolutionary Funding Collaboratory (a program of the Evolutionary Futures Lab)** – For supporting transcontextual action learning for systems transformation through thought leadership and collaborative funding
- **Buddha Mind Monastery** – For spiritual inspiration and continued support

Special Thanks
To every volunteer, community leader, teacher, farmer, and child whose spirit shines through these pages—
Your resilience is the true author of this book.
A heartfelt thanks to the volunteers from Love Africa Mission and to the students and staff of CIYOTA—
Your kindness, collaboration, and spirit of community added immeasurable depth to this journey.

Publishing and Support
Endless gratitude to the family, friends, and global mentors who helped bring this dream to life.

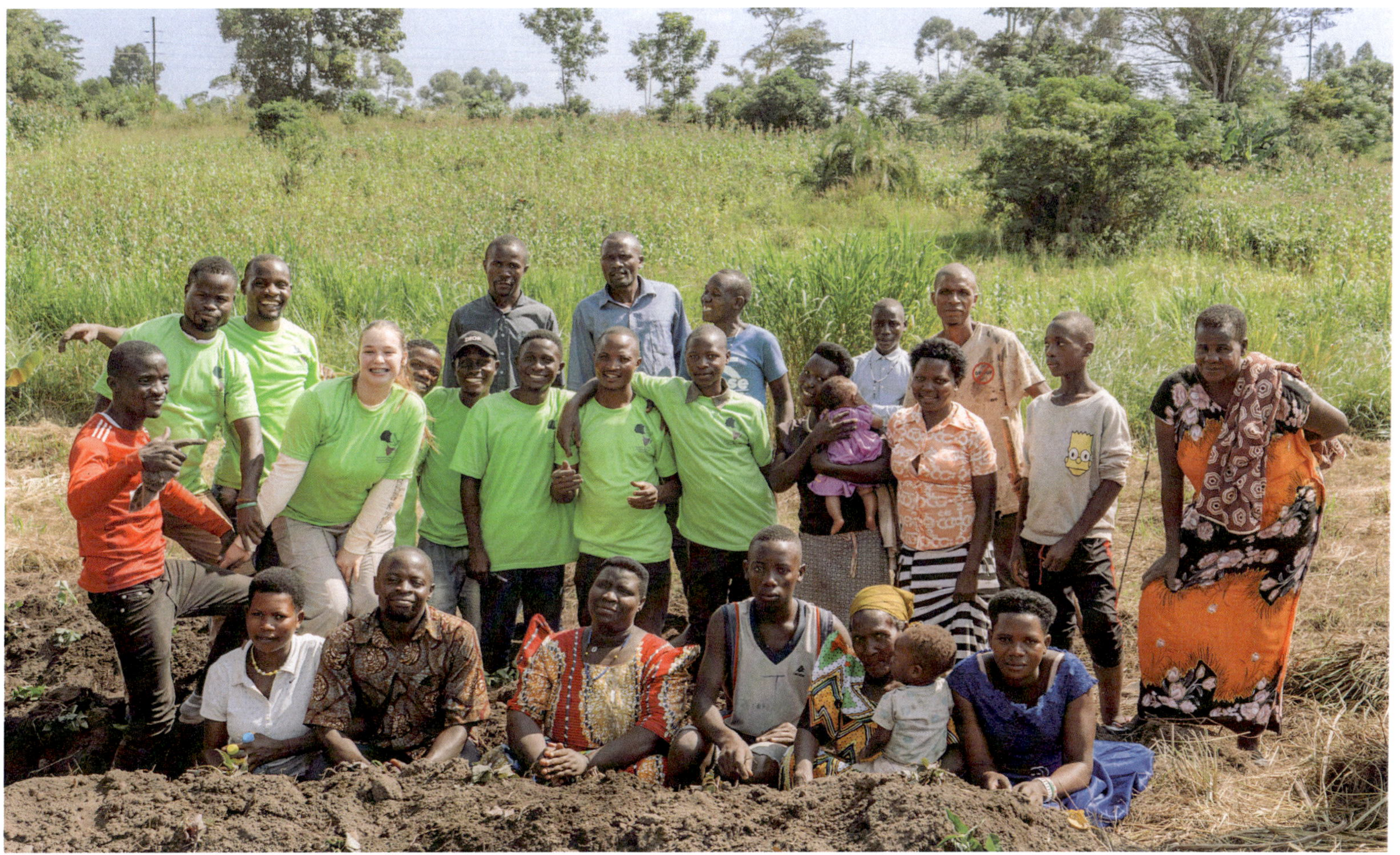

Agri Planet Africa staff, volunteers, and local families at their Community Resource Center—united in vision, rooted in resilience.